Edwin Cone Bissell

Genesis printed in Colors

Showing the original Sources from which it is supposed to have been

compiled

Edwin Cone Bissell

Genesis printed in Colors
Showing the original Sources from which it is supposed to have been compiled

ISBN/EAN: 9783337144258

Printed in Europe, USA, Canada, Australia, Japan

Cover: Foto ©ninafisch / pixelio.de

More available books at **www.hansebooks.com**

GENESIS PRINTED IN COLORS

SHOWING THE ORIGINAL SOURCES FROM
WHICH IT IS SUPPOSED TO HAVE
BEEN COMPILED

WITH AN INTRODUCTION

By EDWIN CONE BISSELL

Professor in McCormick Theological Seminary, Chicago

"Prove all things; hold fast that which is good" — 1 Thess. v. 21

HARTFORD, CONN.
BELKNAP & WARFIELD
1892

INTRODUCTION.

CORRECTIONS IN THE INTRODUCTION.

P. iii, line 14, change "previous" to XVIth; line 27, "lemon" to orange; line 33, "orange" to lemon.

P. v, line 3, change 16, 18, to 16–18; line 20, "verse 27" to verse 46; line 21, "49" to 50.

P. xii, strike out footnote and the reference to it in the text.

the explanations given on the previous page. The blue color, leaning on in the text, represents the supposed original source of the Hexateuch — that is, the Pentateuch and Joshua — generally entitled P. This letter stands for Priests' Code, the most essential part of it being those laws of Exodus, Leviticus, and Numbers, which relate to the priesthood and the "Mosaic" institutions generally. It embraces about one-half of the matter of this part of the Bible. The next color (black), beginning at 2: 4ᵇ is used for a document known as J, the first letter of the word Jehovist, or Jahvist, for which it stands. It is held to be partial, throughout Genesis, to the title *Jehovah* for God, as the previous document is to the word *Elohim*. In the character of its matter it is mostly historical, though with a tendency to prophecy.

The third color (green), first appearing in a single word, likewise in 2: 4ᵇ, is used for every sort of editorial addition and change, early or late, found in any of the alleged sources, including the transference of matter from one source to another. For the indication of glosses, that is, of matter which, after the final redaction, found its way into the text, a black line, as at 2: 19, has been drawn under the matter thus explained. The fourth color (lemon), beginning with 4: 16, does not, by itself, stand for a separate document, but simply for an earlier source of J (J¹). It is a part of the theory of our critics maintaining the analysis, that each of the three principal sources found in Genesis circulated, at first, as an independent work and so became more or less altered before they were combined together in their present form.

For chapter 14, which Kautzsch and Socin felt unable to classify with any of the other documents, a special color (orange) is used. Most critics assign it to the editor who worked it over on the basis of the E document later described. In 15: 1–4, and occasionally afterwards, there is an example of an alleged combination of the two documents J and E in such a manner that they are no longer separable. For matter of this sort a brown color has been chosen. The document E is said to appear, independently, first in chapter 20, though subsequently requiring a good deal of space in Genesis, P largely retiring before it. For E a red color has been selected. Its matter is mostly historical like that of J, and in other respects, it is claimed to have a close affinity with it, though, like P, using the title *Elohim* for God. From this last circumstance it derives its name. As it respects the age of the several sources, there is pretty general, though by no means universal, agreement among those who accept the analysis that their chronological order is J, E, P, and that none of them took fixed form until long after the Mosaic period. The usual date for J and E being about B. C. 800–750; while P is regarded as post-exilian, the publication of it being assigned by Wellhausen to B. C. 444.

Such is the analysis which has been fixed upon for the first book of the Bible. Here our introduction might properly have ended had it seemed likely that this manual would come only into the hands of persons fully acquainted with the discussions which have preceded, and are still going on over this partition of the text. Since this is most improbable, it appeared desirable to note also some of the chief grounds on which the scheme is advocated, together with such other facts as may guide the intelligent reader in his independent investigations and point the way to just results. A beginning may be made then, by inquiring whether on *a priori*

---

[1] *Die Genesis mit Aeusserer Unterscheidung der Quellenschriften, etc.*: Zweite Auflage, Freiburg, 1891.

(iii)

or other grounds it is antecedently probable that so many documentary histories on this theme, and of this sort, would naturally have arisen among the Israelites at the periods named, or at any other period.[1] If this question cannot certainly be negatived, it will be next in order to examine the compilation itself, including, as one goes on, the material of the several documents said to compose it. It is claimed that it consists of very dissimilar matter. In fact, this dissimilarity is one of the chief reasons given for regarding the documents as such. It relates — as in the end will more fully appear — not only to their point of view, but to a host of particulars in which they are found to clash with, and even directly to contradict, one another. It will be in point, accordingly, to ask further, whether such diversity of material might not well have deterred a compiler in that early day from his undertaking. If the answer usually given be accepted as valid and sufficient, that in his time these documents had already and equally attained semi-canonical valuation notwithstanding their mutual antagonisms and that he wished to preserve them as intact as possible, the faithful investigator will still be far from the solution of his problem.

He will take note of the fact, in passing, that it is largely with presuppositions and conjectures that he has thus far had to do. Some of them are of a colossal character and beyond the reach of verification; as, for instance, that these heterogeneous documents passed through several editions before being united together as they now are, and that from this fact arise certain of their present peculiarities (J[1]). He will be moved, therefore, to ask by what process documents, by admission and necessary presupposition, so radically unlike, have been united together to form a literary and ethical unity so remarkable as is acknowledged to exist in the book of Genesis. He will be led, in short, to study, and thoroughly test the method of the compiler. Does he, as matter of fact, treat his material as though it were of a sacred character? Is he everywhere consistent with himself? Is he frank and open in his dealing, and evidently governed by a purpose in harmony with the object he ostensibly has in view? Undoubtedly the best way to understand a book is to come, in some good degree, into sympathy with the man who wrote it.[2] Is it possible to do so with this unknown author of Genesis? These questions, we say, will not be settled by the faithful investigator off-hand, or on merely *a priori* grounds. What he wants is strictly scientific results. He will consequently adopt a proper logical method, and follow the compiler, step by step, throughout his work. The present book offers to him the opportunity of doing this easily. By means of it a reader of ordinary intelligence can readily learn what the supposed original sources are, how they have been dealt with in relation to one another, and what is to be learned besides, through the direct testimony of the matter printed in green, of the spirit and aims of the compiler.

We have no wish to anticipate, much less prejudice, the personal investigations which this manual may inspire. We do consider ourselves, however, at liberty to point out the facts as far as we may be able to do so in our limited space. A recent writer in Germany who accepts the analysis says of this feature of it: "One thing strikes me unpleasantly in the results of the hypothesis of the documents thus far attained, that the acuteness of the supposed redactor stands in absolutely antipodal relations to the cleverness of the critics. The redactor is supposed to have made the compilation according to principles which directly exclude one another. At one time he reproduced his sources with the greatest faithfulness; at another he had reference to the connection and unity of his own work."[3] Professor Harper speaks even more depreciatingly of this theoretical personage in his series of papers in *Hebraica*.[4] He says: "His spirit is far from being a critical one. He did not hesitate to use his material in any way which would best subserve his aim. He inserted and omitted; changed and arranged. He handled the sources used as freely as if he had been the author. Again,[5] "If it," that is, the matter of Genesis, "is composed of different stories of the same event, joined together by an editor who did not have insight sufficient to enable him to see that he was all the time committing grave blunders, and yet felt no hesitation in altering the originals with which he was working, it is not historical in the ordinary sense of that term." These are grave charges, and they are made, be it observed, by critics who hold to the analysis. One says that the compiler was not consistent with himself, but quite the contrary; the other, that he is uncritical, without adequate capacity, committing all the time grave blunders, and, worst of all, that he is untrue to the originals with which he worked. It is for the reader himself to test the matter whether these complaints have just grounds and how far they represent the true state of the case.

We may refer, for example, to 7: 3, 9, 23 where, in three instances, without note or comment, he has inserted in one of his authorities words taken bodily from another; and point out that in doing so he is acting in direct antagonism with the principle which, in general, is sup-

---

[1] See *Biblia* for Aug., 1891. p. 126; also Prof. Osgood in the same (a reprinted paper from the *S. S. Times*) for Jan., p. 123.
[2] See Robertson, in the *Baird Lecture* for 1891, p. vii.
[3] Volk, *Entwickelungsgeschichte der A. T. Religion*, 1891. p. 12.   [4] V. 68.   [5] *Ibid.*, p. 70.

INTRODUCTION.

posed to govern him, that his documents are canonically sacred and are allowed to speak for themselves. Other efforts to smooth over abrupt transitions, or to supply additional information by the insertion of extraneous matter appear in 9: 18, 19; 10: 9, 16,–18, 24. In 12: 17, he has without authority added the words "and his house." In 13: 1, he has likewise altered the documentary record by inserting "and Lot with him." In 15: 7, 8, 12–16, 19–21, he has introduced a large amount of matter into what was originally a simple account of a sacrifice by Abraham, giving a wholly different meaning to the transaction. In 16: 8–10, there is another attempt at harmonizing conflicting statements by supplying words which are put into the mouths of Hagar and of Jehovah. In 17: 10, there is a similar insertion of unauthorized material, and here, in what purports to be a direct promise from God to Abraham. In 21: 1, and in 22: 11, he has changed the word *Elohim* to *Jehovah*. In the latter chapter he is also responsible for verses 14–18, i. e., for the important promises of Jehovah to Abraham and the naming of the place where he offered Isaac, "Jehovah-jireh." In verse 20 he is guilty of a gross chronological misstatement by putting in the words, "after these things," which, if real, belong elsewhere and to another document. In 24: 67, he has deliberately inserted the misleading words "his mother" and "his mother Sarah." In 26: 1, he asserts what he must have known to be untrue, that the famine there described was a different one from that which occurred in the days of Abraham; and the context contains three other falsifications of the record (verses 2–5, 15, 18), to make them square with the first. To make a smoother transition between chapters 27 and 28, and give an appearance of continuity, he forged verse 27 of the former. In place of *Jehovah* he put *Elohim* in 31: 49. Again, to give the appearance of a continuous narrative where there was, in fact, merely a two-fold account of the same event, he inserted the word "again" in 35: 9. Throughout the history of Joseph (37: 5, 8, 10; 39: 1, 8, 10, 20, 23; 42: 7, 28; 43: 14; 45: 19–21; 46: 1, 3, 5, 8–27; 47: 4, 24; 48: 7, 21; 49: 28; 50: 22), he did apparently his best by arbitrary insertions, changing proper names, transferring matter from one source to another, and other, as from the basis of the theory must be allowed, unwarrantable alterations to produce from his threefold originals of the one story a pleasing verisimilitude which should pass for truth.[1]

Now these are facts which are matter of record by our critics on the pages before us, and no one of them cares to dispute them. It is for the intelligent reader to say what their real bearing is on the current theory of the analysis which they are meant to support. It is not needful, at present, to consider, unless one so choose, what their bearing is on the important questions of the authenticity, authority, and divine inspiration of Genesis; but how are they supposed to help the theory under consideration? Do they help it, or are they a millstone about its neck? One can see how our critics might suppose themselves to be benefited by this conspicuous ally; though he often acts in alleged antagonism with himself; yes, especially, because he so acts. It increases by so much — does it not ? — the realm of possible conjecture in which they must be acknowledged so largely to move. The list of passages in which they agree with what he is supposed to have done is by no means small. Those in which they disagree with him extend, so much further, the area of supposition, and, what is more, permit in the material another sort of adjustment to the main theory, which from the usual point of view would be impossible. The discriminating reader is to decide, then, since our critics themselves have not told us what their real object was in suggesting such a device, whether it was not intended to give them a chance, in certain necessary cases, to guess twice instead of once. Who is the redactor? Is he, or is he not, the creature of the theory which makes use of him? Can it, by any possibility, be maintained without him; without *him*, the blunderer, the confessedly inconsistent and uncritical compiler, a litterateur without capacity and often, at least, without honesty, who yet set for himself the task of preparing a sacred history of the world's beginning and of God's ways with men ? "Science implies some system of presentation, some consistency of views, some coherence of reasoning." Does it require it less in the immediate agent than in the principal? *Qui facit per alium facit per se.*

The matter just considered may, or may not, be regarded as decisive of the main question at issue. It is, however, but one of many tests to be applied to the reasoning of our critics of the analysis. There are chiefly four grounds on which they base the conclusions to which they have come: alleged duplicate, or triplicate accounts of the same event; differences in point of view relating to theological and other matters; and diversity in style and vocabulary, including the use of the divine names. As yet there has been no adequate presentation, by English or American writers, of these several arguments.[2] The scheme has made its *début* among us as a product of the "ripest German scholarship," and has been generally accepted, if at all, on the basis of what is commonly known as the "consensus of later criticism." In the most of what

---

[1] We have taken the liberty here of quoting matter, to some extent, from a paper of our own in the *Hartford Seminary Record* for Oct., 1891, p. 4.
[2] The series of papers by Drs. Harper and Green in *Hebraica*, from Oct., 1888, is unlikely to reach, unfortunately, a large circle of readers in their present form.

has appeared on the subject, "there is a continual assumption of something which the reader has been no party in establishing, a building upon foundations which are underground. Whether the assumptions are supported by arguments to which he would yield, whether the foundations are securely laid, he does not know. He must, therefore, either surrender himself to his critical guides, or get perplexed over the mass of intricate details."[1] All that can be hoped for in the present essay, as has been said, is to put the reader in the way of settling for himself, without undue bias from any quarter, the leading points in the discussion.

Taking up, severally, the arguments named, though in a reverse order, it is obvious that there is a somewhat peculiar use of the divine names *Elohim* and *Jehovah* in the earlier chapters of Genesis; and it is not strange that it suggested, long ago, the possibility of different documentary sources. The careful reader will find, however, that this peculiarity is confined to the earlier portions. In the last ten chapters of the book the title *Jehovah* occurs but once, a fact, apparently, which has little influence on the analysis adopted. It should be stated, indeed, that this usage respecting the divine names in Genesis has, at present, compared with earlier periods of the criticism, quite a subordinate place. It is for the reader to say whether it is especially singular that different names, expressive of different relations, are applied to God in the Bible, or that relatively more is made of this fact, as of the meaning of other proper names, in its opening pages. It will be noted that the compiler evidently wishes to be understood as putting *Jehovah* quite on a level with *Elohim* (see chaps. 2, 3). It will be noted, too, that the theory before us presupposes that while the document J had both titles at its disposal, it uses, predominantly, one of them. Is not, then, the principle tacitly assumed by our critics themselves, that, in the case of one of these early writers, at least, the significance of the title had much to do with its special use? Furthermore, were it to be admitted as probable that the alternation of the divine titles in the early chapters of Genesis of itself points towards a theory of two original sources, should it not be expected, on every ground, that *Elohim* would be found with the older one? Above all, ought not *Jehovah* to have been the title dominating in the Priests' code and the "Mosaic" institutions generally? The reader will certainly not fail to see the injustice in such a discussion of putting at the start a new interpretation on Ex. 6: 3, coeval only with the theory it is made to support, to the effect that the name *Jehovah* was unknown in the patriarchal period.[2]

These preliminary considerations being duly weighed, an inductive study of the use of the divine names in Genesis will be in order. Unless the critical reader arrive at different results from those obtained by us, he will be struck with the ease with which the two chiefly concerned range themselves under the following heads, no one of which is unreasonable or out of harmony with the theory of the essential unity of the book. 1. The distinction in usage is sometimes based on the natural difference between God as creator and ruler in nature, and God in human history, or as theocratic ruler. 2. *Jehovah* is used not only in harmony with the principle just stated, but, at the same time, in immediate connection with other divine names on their first introduction, for the purpose of identification (as *Elohim* in chapters 2, 3; *El Elyon*, 14: 22; *El Shaddai*, 17: 1). This usage is very instructive in many respects. 3. *Elohim* is often used appellatively (= Deity): to mark the distinction between God and man as such (as at 5: 22), or in connection with those outside the theocracy (as at 3: 2). 4. One or the other title is used on the ground that, for some one of the above reasons, it has been used in a previous section, to which evident, though tacit, reference is thus made. 5. They are *occasionally* interchanged for one another, in the last two-thirds of the book, for no specially apparent reason, either title being appropriate in the circumstances.

On the other hand, it will occasion no little surprise, that the current theory which sets out really *to explain* this literary phenomenon, among many others, has so much difficulty even in adjusting itself to it. Besides the numerous instances where *Elohim* is allowed — illogically we must think — to remain in the *Jehovah* document on the ground that it does not concern the analysis (in addition to twenty times in Chapters 2 and 3, with *Jehovah*, *cf.* 3: 1, 3, 5; 4: 25; 6: 2, 4; 9: 27 (J); 32: 29, 31; 39: 9; 44: 16) it is necessary to invoke the aid of the redactor directly to change the title *Elohim* to *Jehovah* or, *vice versa*, seven times (7: 9; 14: 22; 17: 1 (most critics); 21: 1; 22: 11; 28: 21; 31: 50; *cf. Jehovah* in E 39: 5); and, indirectly, that is, by excerpting fragments of the text from their natural context thirteen times

---

[1] Robertson, *ibid.*, p. 4.
[2] That this cannot be the meaning of the passage may be shown from several considerations. 1. Its actual use in the narrative from the beginning of Genesis is against it; particularly in Ex. 3: 14, where a similar emphasis is given to its etymological meaning. 2. Ex. 6: 3, refers, especially, as is clear from its language, to Gen. 17: 1. But in this very verse *Jehovah* is used for God, and the point can only be evaded by referring it to the redactor, as is done by the most of our critics. 3. Giving the Hebrew word *to know* in this place its usual meaning as in the Bible in such a connection, the statement signifies simply that God was not understood, appreciated by the Patriarchs in his character as *Jehovah*. The distinction, as so often, is quantitative not qualitative. 4. There are still other passages in Genesis, besides 17: 1, where *Jehovah* is found in the P document (where it should not be if the theory be true), and has to be removed by the same violent method, or the fact met by hypotheses equally unsupported and improbable (*cf.* 5: 29; 7: 16; 21: 1). 5. If Ex. 6: 3, assert what our critics claim, it asserts too much for them, *viz.*: that God was known to the Patriarchs only (or, at least, chiefly) under the name *El Shaddai*, while they hold that the name commonly used was *Elohim*.

INTRODUCTION.

(5:29; 7:16; 19:29; 20:18; 21:1, 33; 22:14-18; 27:28; 30:24, 27; 31:3; 33:5, 11). If the reader find these data correct, he will draw his own conclusions as to their bearing on the current theory. Textual emendation is the last resort of the critic. The number of such emendations or accommodations here, would, no doubt, have greatly shocked an Astruc or an Eichhorn, who were the first to use the present argument in favor of different original sources. Another pretty clear result of such an inductive study of the divine names in Genesis relates to chapters 20-50. It is absolutely needful for the theory to assume here the existence of a second *Elohim* document. But it appears that it largely takes the place of P, which uses this title elsewhere; while, at the same time, it is confessedly so much like its companion document J, in material and diction, that not a few of our critics, as is well known, declare themselves unable or unwilling to draw the line between them.

The argument from language outside the divine names requires extreme care for obvious reasons. It is admitted to be relatively weak, and can never have more than a subordinate and supplementary value.[1] There is no visible cleavage line among the supposed sources. Certain sections, or passages, which show certain features are assigned to one document, and those which are left, to another, or two others. And presto! the sources appear. Could any other result have been expected, or well be possible? The foregone conclusion, in each case, has been assumed as a premise, and used as a part of the argument. We need not suppose that such a process of reasoning has been consciously adopted. But it is next to impossible in the present instance, or indeed in any branch of the argument for documents under these circumstances, to avoid this logical snare. Of course, if it be found in the end that certain sections, or passages, agree together over against certain others, in a number of different particulars, such as language and style, point of view and form of presentation, a presumption would arise that they had a different origin. One would, however, be far from having a scientific proof of it. In the nature of the case, it must forever remain with such data an open question whether the several passages had been correctly distributed.

The following principles, it is hoped, will commend themselves to the candid reader as fitted to guide him in the further examination of this branch of the subject. 1. Words and expressions cited as characteristic of a supposed original document should be of a marked character in themselves, and be used sufficiently often to be properly so named. If they are seldom found, and found in one portion of the document only, why may not that fact be as validly used to disprove the unity of the document as the unity of the work? 2. On the supposition that language is used to express a writer's thoughts, the subject-matter in which supposed characteristic expressions are found is always to be given the predominant place in deciding why they were used. 3. Any number of alleged peculiar words and expressions, including grammatical forms, found in one set of passages in comparison with others where they do not appear, should obviously be given no consideration in determining the question of original sources, unless at the same time it is shown that there was just occasion for their use in both. 4. The fact that certain words, expressions, and grammatical forms occur oftener in one alleged document than in another cannot fairly be given weight in settling the question of the existence of such documents until after it has been shown in detail that there was a fair opportunity for their use the same number of times in each. This test may impose no little additional labor on the critic; but without it all his other labor is clearly in vain.

5. It should be determined whether, in solving the problem of documents, words and expressions shall be considered which, in order to have a bearing, must be subjected to the strain of a double conjecture: as, for example, in addition to the original one, that they are not in their original form, but have been changed by the editor; or that they are not in their original place, when to remove them would be seriously to impair the present sense of the passage. 6. In cases where synonyms for the same, or a similar, thought are used, it is to be decided whether the same shade of meaning was intended by the writer, or writers; and, if so, whether the use of the synonym is more likely to be due to a different writer, or to the common habit in Hebrew writers of clothing their thoughts in a variety of forms. 7. Great care is to be taken to be just to the material as a whole, which is to be examined. Over against words and expressions supposed to be peculiar to two or more documents, respectively, there should be a thorough search to see whether there is not an equal, or even a greater, number common to both, or all, and peculiar to them. If this should be found to be the case, and one still hold to the current hypothesis of documents, would he not be compelled to conclude, either that they quote one another, or that both, or all, look back to a common original work on which they depend?[2] 8. Words of legislative or ritualistic coloring found in P

---

[1] See *Hebraica*, V. 24, 64.
[2] A few of the results to be obtained by such a study may be indicated. The following words or expressions found in both P and J (or E) have at least a footing in Genesis: flesh (6:3), create (2:4b), lift up the hand (form of oath, implied in 14:22; cf. Ex. 6:8; Nu. 14:30), name (=fame 12:2), shekel, half shekel (23:15; 24:22), said to his heart (*i. e.*, within himself, 8:21; 17:17), heavens and earth (1:1), set time (17:21; 18:14), article with the *Inf. estr.* (2:9), journeyings (13:3), towards, away from, the sea (=west, 12:8), shortened form of the demonstrative pronoun *pd.* (19:8),

might fail to appear in J or E on the reasonable ground that they have no legislative material save Ex. xx.–xxiii. So, too, poetic expressions should not be expected where, in the nature of the case, or because of a previous manipulation of the material, there is no poetry. 9. Words may be found in several places in Genesis because of the mutual interdependence of the sections in their thought and a tacit reference of one to the other, rather than because they characterize a separate document. 10. There must be obtained, at the outset, the widest possible *consensus* of our critics respecting the bounds of the supposed documents. For example, a large proportion of the words said to be characteristic of P are found in Chapter 1.

But we are told, at the same time, by our critics, that there is no unanimity in making this chapter original with P.[1] This is the more important, that P is said to have a very limited historical vocabulary, the same becoming practically exhausted before Genesis is more than two-thirds completed.[2] 11. Since it is inherently probable, and generally admitted by critics of all schools that to some degree original sources were used, by the author of Genesis, it is not to be forthwith concluded, if an examination of its language and style show the likelihood of such use, that the current theory of compilation is the correct one. The theory adopted must square itself to the actual facts as they shall appear.[3] Let, now, these evidently just principles of criticism be wisely and conscientiously followed and something approaching probability may be expected as a result in this department of the investigation. A desire to keep this paper within reasonable limits and to avoid, as far as possible, the technic of the classroom, prevents our making here an application of them in detail. Let it suffice to say that, axiomatic and reasonable as they may seem, their effect will be found exceedingly drastic on the formidable-looking lists of words adduced by our critics as characteristic of the several documents.

The next point to be considered is one closely connected with the last: an alleged difference of style in the supposed documents, especially between P and J (or E). P's style is said to be stiff, statistical, chronological, and to abound in repetitions; while J's is free, flowing, and even, at times, poetic. It should be noted that difference of style — in distinction from vocables — between J and E is not emphasized; and, again, that it is not until a division has been made between P and J on the ground of style, among other things, that this argument is plied. Chapter I, admitted to be wholly unique, even lapidarian in its style, and all the numerous and extended genealogies are first assigned to one of the documents, and the most of the narrative (and poetic) matter to the other. Then attention is called to their differences. To be fair, the comparison should be made among different sections of the text under like conditions, when both have the same theme and the same purpose: as, for example, in the account of the flood. As it is, the remark of Dr. Green seems fully justified: "With the same propriety a bill presented by a merchant to his customer might be compared with a letter written to his wife, and diversity of authorship inferred, because one deals in dates and figures and business forms, and the other in easy, flowing sentences."[4]

The third principal argument used in support of the current analysis is an alleged difference among the several sources in point of view. As hitherto, only a bare example of the reasoning *pro* and *con* can be given. It is claimed that J — with which E may here be included — is much more anthropomorphic than P, is less clear and firm in its monotheism; represents God as on familiar terms with men, appears to him, and the like; in short, betrays an earlier and more mythical coloring than P. It likewise anticipates, early in Genesis, the later Levitical laws: lets Cain and Abel sacrifice; gives directions about altars; prohibits cer-

---

living (applied to water, 26: 19), the three principal synonyms for swearing (12; 3; 24: 41; 27: 12, *etc.*), a peculiar form of a common word for sheep (30: 33), a peculiar word for trader (34: 10), the two principal synonyms for staff (32: 11; 38: 18), a very rare compound preposition (38: 24), a word for fine linen for which another was used during and after the Exile (41: 42), the short form of the 1st person *pl.* of the personal pronoun (42: 11), according to the mouth of the little ones (= ac. to the size of the family. 47: 12). The list might be greatly and fairly extended, especially, by including words and expressions really common to both, but given exclusively to one or the other through the redactor (6; 7; 7: 3, *etc.*).

[1] *Hebraica*, iv. 220, v. 21.   [2] *Ibid.*, v. 286.   Chapters 2 and 3 of Genesis, too, assigned generally to J, and made largely its standard, are denied to it by eminent critics.

[3] Nobody now holds, as far as we know, that Moses, or any one else, originally composed Genesis, *verbatim et literatim*, just as we now have it. All scholars regard it as probable that whoever wrote it had, for some parts of it, documentary sources. The elder Delitzsch used, in his classes, to express it as his opinion that Abraham, when he entered Canaan, brought with him from his eastern home, written, as well as oral, narratives covering the facts of the earlier parts of Genesis. He could not well have failed to be informed of such facts, since transcripts of them in polytheistic form appeared on the monuments of his native land. It is also a fact of significance that in the Akkadian account of the Deluge, Hasisadra, who represents the Biblical Noah, is said to have been ordered to bury certain documents before entering the ark. There is another, and a perfectly legitimate method, accordingly, for accounting for some peculiarities of language and style in the opening chapters of the Bible without resorting to the wide-reaching and all-inclusive theory of our critics. It is pretty generally conceded, moreover, that, whatever isolated exceptions there may be to the rule, as a rule the language of Genesis is the oldest extant form of the Hebrew. On one hand the book is characterized by a considerable number of archaistic expressions, if the language have any. On the other, it is equally marked by a conspicuous absence of signs of a late age (*cf.* Ryssel, *De Elohistæ Pentateuchici Sermone*, Lips., 1878; Dillmann, Die Buecher Numeri, Deuteronomium, *etc.*, 1886, pp. 663-665). If, therefore, from the criterion of language and style alone, it is impossible to say that the book did not arise in the time of the early kings of Israel, B. C. 1000-750, it is equally impossible to deny that it might have arisen in the times of Moses.

[4] *Hebraica*, v. 286. Tuch (*Com. Uber die Genesis*, p. xlix.) says of P: "Die Schreibart im letzteren Theile (wird) geschmiediger und flüssiger als sie zu Anfange erscheint."

tain abuses of worship, presupposes the arts of civilized life, and so on, all of which is not only foreign to P, but impossible to it as being of much later origin.[1] Looking at the other side, it should not be unnoticed by the discriminating reader that P has relatively but a small amount of matter in Genesis, in which such themes would naturally be treated. It is, as we have seen, largely genealogical, and otherwise of a formal character. The sections assigned to J, on the contrary, in the nature of the case, that is, because *Jehovah* predominates in them, might be expected to be relatively more didactic, predictive, and anthropomorphic.

It might also be expected to contain most of what relates to the early forms of worship and the practices of Patriarchal religion. It is *Jehovah* who specially represents God as he appears in Revelation and in human history, and, hence, it is he who comes into the closest relations with men. Still, it will appear, on closer examination, that P is *as really* anthropomorphic as J (cf. 1: 3, 4, 5). The question of more or less is unimportant in view of the fact that neither goes beyond, if it parallels, similar expressions in the Prophets (Is. 7: 18) and the Psalms (14: 2; 44: 24). If, moreover, J is held not to be rigidly monotheistic because it represents God as saying, "Let us go down"; "The man has become as one of us" (3: 22; 4: 7); then, by parity of reasoning, is not P involved in the same charge according to whom God says: "Let us make man in our image"; or Isaiah who puts into the mouth of God the words (6: 8): "Whom shall I send, and who will go for us?" In P, too, we are told of Noah and Enoch that they "walked" with God; and of Abraham, that he "talked" with him. In P there is the same sort of theophany implied as is described in J, when it is said that *Elohim* "went up" from Abraham; "went up" from Jacob after communing with them (17: 22; 35: 13). It is conceded that passages ascribed to J *foreshadow* (*presuppose* they do not), in some respects, subsequent Mosaic laws, speak of sacrifices and altars, *etc.* But it will be found that these facts betoken, both in circumstances and form, an earlier stage in the history. Besides, passages in P do as much as this also. It is P which furnishes the basis for the future law of the Sabbath (2: 1); introduces and emphasizes the rite of circumcision (17: 10, 11); prohibits the eating of blood, and so looks directly forward to the law of sacrifice (9: 4); recognizes the separation between Israel and the nations, of which so much is made in the later law (Chapter 34); and, unless the text be changed to avoid it, itself recognizes the custom of the drink-offering and of anointing a pillar with oil (35: 13, 14.)[2] Undoubtedly, in the matter referred to J (J¹) the rise of the arts and a general application of them is indicated (4: 16-24; 11: 1-9); but it should not have been overlooked that a similar knowledge is implied in P in its account of Noah's experience with the Ark (6: 13-16). Hence, the question left to the reader who faithfully follows throughout the book the course suggested is, Do the facts really warrant the conclusion reached? Is there a sufficient difference between P and J in these respects, all the circumstances being considered, to justify, so far, the theory of separate documents?

The fourth and final argument principally urged in support of the current view of the composition of Genesis is that there are evidently found in it variant accounts of one and the same series of events, with many needless repetitions, betraying to the critical observer the secret of its origin. We come here to what appears to be a more tangible, and appreciable reason than any which has preceded it. But the duty of proving all things and holding fast only that which is good is no less imperative than ever. To begin at the beginning, there are, it is claimed, two radically distinct accounts of the creation (Gen. 1-2: 4ᵃ; 2: 4ᵇ-23), resulting from the juxtaposition of the two principal documents of Genesis. One, P, represents the creation as proceeding from lower to higher forms of life; J, the reverse; in P there is too much water for vegetation; in J, too little; in P man and woman were created together; in J the order is man, vegetation, animals, woman; in P man is given supreme authority over the earth at once; in J he attains it only after sin and punishment; in P man is created in God's image to rule over the earth; in J it is a sin for man to seek to be as God, to know the world; in P the universe is conceived of as a "diving-bell" in water; in J the earth is an indefinite extent of dry plain on which the water must be poured by Jehovah.

The supposed history contained in chapters four and five of Genesis is similarly decomposed and precipitated by the chemical tests of the criticism. There are two distinct and variously discrepant narratives covering the same ground (J: chap. 4, except 16ᵇ-24; P: chap. 5, except verse 28, "a son," and verse 29). The genealogies, though represented in the text as showing different lines, are really the same thing in different forms. By blunder or caprice they have become attached to different ancestors. The document J appears extremely weak compared with its neighbor. Its anthropomorphisms are said to be excessive. It makes Jehovah assist at child-birth, have a heated discussion with Cain, represents that Cain should have had more knowledge than he exhibits concerning sacrifice. The narrative of the flood

---

[1] It will be seen how readily, from constant practice (?) our critics slip into the fallacy known as *circulus in probando*. Cf. *Hebraica*, v. 50, *et passim*.
[2] Kautzsch and Socin (foot-note *in loco*) offer the same reason for calling in the redactor here, of which so great use is made elsewhere; it is not like P to speak of such things, and so he does not here. But that is the point in dispute.

x *INTRODUCTION.*

(Gen., chaps. 6-9), is claimed to show in a marked degree evidence of the combination of duplicate accounts. According to P, the beginning of the flood is dated by the life of Noah (7: 6, 11, 13); it is caused by convulsions of nature; the waters prevail one hundred and fifty days; they disappear and the earth is dry after two months (8: 13ᵃ, 14). According to J the flood is announced but seven days before its appearance (7: 4, 10); the rain was on the earth forty days and nights; the ground dries up after one hundred and one days (8: 6, 8, 10, 12, 13ᵇ). P's ark has a window system and a door in the side; J's has a window and a cover. J's distinction between clean and unclean animals is foreign to P. J makes the flood local and limited; P, universal.

So throughout the account of the patriarchs there is the same duplication of material and dubiety of impression, until we come to the twentieth chapter of Genesis, when the confusion is increased by the use of the new document (E) containing still another version of the events narrated. Did Abraham have any quarrels in his family or not (Abraham with Lot, Sarah with Hagar)? Did Sarah actually go down with him into Egypt? The associated authorities differ on these points. Can circumcision be dated from Abraham's time? The older document knows nothing of it. The facts concerning Hagar and Ishmael are particularly muddled by the two stories. By one, Ishmael being unborn, Hagar is so treated that she flees; by the other, she is driven out with the child on her shoulder. (!) By one, Hagar is at fault; by the other, it is Ishmael. The record, moreover, is inconsistent in representing that Ishmael is carried on the shoulder at all; since he is too old to be so treated (P and J, 16: 1-16, except 8-10, R; E 21: 8-21). The representation of a two-fold covenant with Abraham (chaps. 15 and 17) is likewise false. It is the same event twice described, and the differences, which are by no means few, it is necessary to charge, as so often before, to the account of profit and loss. Double, and sometimes triple, reasons are given for proper names as that of Ishmael (J 16: 11, 12; P 17: 18, 21), of Isaac (P 17: 17; J 18: 12; E 21: 6), of Edom (J 25: 25; 25: 30), of several of Jacob's sons, of Mahanaim, Penuel, and of Israel (J 32: 25-32; P 35: 10); although it is assumed that but one of them, if either, is correct; and so on, to the end of Genesis, and the end of the Hexateuch.

Here, as before, the uppermost and the final question now before the inquirer does not concern so much the authenticity and inspiration of the narrative, but the facts of its origin. Still the two questions cannot be kept wholly apart. The examination of the alleged phenomena at this point, accordingly, will be as searching as the importance of the subject requires. The serious-minded will wish to know how it is that such a host of supposed discrepancies and contradictions have come into being for the first time just now. If they inhere in the text, by what literary artifice did the redactor, this redactor whose capacity, spirit, and methods have already been characterized, succeed so well in covering them up? The current theory, in one of its earlier stages went literally to pieces by pushing to an extreme the hypothesis of fragments. Is there here, possibly, a near approach to a like catastrophe? Somebody, surely, has blundered egregiously. We have Genesis in its present form. We know clearly enough what its author meant to teach. The value of such teaching cannot be belittled by naming it "traditional." Before rejecting the "tradition," that is, the Biblical narrative of Genesis in its present form, as false, one should be sure that the product of the theory which it is proposed to substitute for it is true; or, at least, less false. The almost indescribable confusion of thought and appalling waste of material necessitated by the current analysis, suggests, on its face, the likelihood of an incorrect method. It is, in fact, a *reductio ad absurdum*.[1] Our critics would hardly confess that they start with the premise that the historical matter of Genesis is practically valueless; quite the contrary. Their conclusion, however, comes to that, and is consequently absurd. A conclusion which requires the falsity of one's premise is, in logic, impossible.

As preliminary to a more detailed examination of the reasoning from supposed variant accounts the following questions are in point: Does any one of the supposed documents, by itself, offer a fairly complete and self-consistent history of events? If not, are the gaps which need to be conjecturally filled the exception or are they the rule? To what extent, if at all, does the analysis seem to be made for the purpose of getting material, or under the stress of needing material for presupposed documents, rather than on the ground that actual documents appear and demand recognition?[2] The matter, in general, as it lies before us outside the alleged main sources (P, J, E,)—how much is there of it? Why just these divisions? If the redactor counts as two, one when he agrees, and another when he disagrees with our

---

[1] A newspaper tells us of a farmer in one of our Western states who, a year since, started a man out on the range with a flock of sheep. Recently he received the following from him: "If you want me to remain here any longer, you'll have to get another flock of sheep; them's all gone."

[2] Here the method of procedure in connection with the life of Abraham is instructive. To bridge over disconnected material in chapters 11-17, six verses and parts of three others need to be rent, severally, from their natural context in J and referred to P (12: 1ᵇ, 5; 13: 6, 11ᵇ, 12ᵃ; 16: 1ᵃ, 3, 15, 16). Note the same process in the life of Joseph (chapter 37 throughout, etc.), a single verse being once divided among four sources (37: 2).

critics, what is to be said of J and E when found apart and when found together? What is to be thought of this entire extraneous matter, in short, as it affects the theory? Is it here because the theory requires it? If so, how can so much scaffolding be justified for what proves, in the end, to be so small a building?

Such inquiries, however, result as they may, do not excuse one from a candid examination of the argument before us in detail. It must suffice here to do this in two conspicuous cases: the narrative of the Creation and that of the Flood. There are by admission no examples of the theory which are more favorable to it. The supposition is, as has been stated, that 2: 4^b-23 is a duplicate of 1-2: 4^a. But it will be observed that the second passage *professes*, by its proper title (2: 4^a), *to be a sequel* to the first; to supplement, rather than duplicate it. ("These are the generations" *etc.*) By uniform usage in Genesis (5: 1; 6: 9, *etc.*) these words refer to descent, not to origin; that is, they call attention here to the matter which follows as being of the nature of a consequent to what precedes. Our critics are obliged, accordingly, in order to adjust the facts to their theory, contrary to usage, to connect these words with the P document which precedes, and to suppose that, originally, they stood at the beginning of chapter 1, where, if used in their ordinary meaning, they would make nonsense. It will be observed, further, that, as matter of fact — the reader is to decide for himself whether this is not the case — the contents of chapter 2 do supplement and complete those of chapter 1. It cannot be maintained, as asserted, that chapter 2, in opposition to chapter 1, presents a different order of the first creation of plants and animals. In harmony with Hebrew style, it rather takes up and expands a matter of prime importance previously introduced.

It is the creation and destiny of man which is the goal in both chapters; though the point of view is different. Let the account of man's creation in 1: 27 be compared with its fuller explanation and expansion in 2: 20-25. How, indeed, could the contents of chapter 3 be understood without just the link which chapter 2 supplies? What need have we of supposing that the order of presentation in chapter 2 (man, vegetables, animals, woman) is intended to be chronological? May it not just as well, may it not far better, on every ground, be due to a natural association of ideas? That this is the correct view is directly confirmed by the fact that what is said of vegetation in chapter 2 has a local coloring simply; relates to the products of the garden in which man was placed. While the animal creation is introduced, apparently, in order to add the new fact that they were brought to man to be named. Over against such an entirely natural explanation of the phenomena involved, is it likely, is it reasonable or even credible, that two different accounts of the creation, which in so many essential particulars would flatly contradict one another, were placed side by side on the opening pages of the Bible?

In the narrative of the flood, the critical method, in general, may be more fully illustrated. At its beginning a bit of supposed extraneous matter is found (J^1). Why is it so regarded? Is it not because it will not adjust itself to the plan of division proposed? It is claimed that it ignores the flood, although ostensibly an introduction to it; and that it limits human life, thereafter, to 120 years. Here then is an example of what is spoken of by Volk, where the "acuteness of the supposed redactor stands in absolutely antipodal relations to the cleverness of the critics." But suppose that the 120 years, as the context requires, refer to the respite to be given to that generation *before the coming of the flood!* It would, to be sure, necessitate a chronological reference in J which is contrary to a common presupposition; but it would also shield the responsible author of Genesis from the charge of self-stultification. Moreover, if this scrap cannot be worked into the present scheme of documents, it does furnish an important link in the literary unity of Genesis. It provides, in fact, just the ethical basis which we might expect for the universality of the flood. Chapters 4 and 5 tell us of the moral degeneracy of Cain's descendants only. Here it is shown that the same was true of Seth's. In other words, there is good and sufficient reason for being satisfied with the present form of the text.

As it respects the narrative which follows, it is claimed, as we have already intimated, that two entirely distinct accounts are — not blended together, but — imbedded, built in, as distinct blocks and capable of being still easily separated from one another. Attention must again be called to so remarkable a literary phenomenon. Two flood stories, originating, according to the theory, hundreds of years apart, and literally swarming with differences and contradictions, some of which we have indicated, when brought together by an editor without essential change, are found to fit one another, like so many serrated blocks, and to form, united, a consecutive history whose unity, with constant use for millenniums, has been undisputed till our day. Is this coincidence, or is it miracle? But let us take a closer look. We shall find no loosely joined, independent sections, but mutually dependent parts of one whole. An occasional overlapping of ideas, a repetition for emphasis, or enlargement, in complete harmony with Hebrew style, there undoubtedly is. But there is also a marked logical interdependence and sequence of thought wholly inconsistent with the theory proposed.

Let the reader test, what J's story would be alone. Beginning it has none; no preliminary announcement of the catastrophe; no command to make preparations; no report of Noah's attitude. It opens abruptly, but seven days before the event, with an order to Noah to enter the ark. The word has the article. It says nothing of the breaking up of the fountains of the great deep, but only reports the wholly insufficient forty days of rain (7: 12); nothing of the stranding of the ark on Ararat (8: 4); nor of the disembarking of Noah and his family — a truly serious omission — nor of the covenant, with its rainbow symbol (9: 13); nor of the blessing pronounced upon Noah and his sons. And so P's story, taken by itself, would be equally incomplete. It has no warning for the Patriarch when he is to enter the ark; no reference to the significant closing of the door; the descending rain, the despatching of the birds (8: 7-11); the removal of the vessel's covering; to Noah's sacrifice and the divine pleasure in it. These are each and all essential elements of the narrative. They are only furnished by the two documents as combined. Without their combination, moreover, the chronology of the flood on which such constant emphasis is laid, is in total confusion; with it there is an orderly succession of events, not only harmonious with itself, but *a priori* reasonable.

As to alleged discrepancies in other respects, they appear, as we have seen to be true in other cases, only after the text is rent asunder. The lighting system of the one does not exclude the one window of the other; nor the covering for the roof, the door in the side. Without the door for which one document alone is made responsible, how is it supposed that the occupants of the ark got in and out of it ? If objects are thrown out of their due perspective, as in a mirage, it need surprise no one, if they appear distorted and grotesque.

Let there be noted, especially, the ocular proof we have in our book of the violence done to the text by our critics. How, for example, is disagreement in the chronology shown ? Only by what is known, in critical parlance, as "cooking" the documents. Look at 7: 17, where a statement on this subject is boldly referred to P, though found in the midst of J. The same is true of vs. 24 and of 8: 13. So at 7: 17, why is the expression "forty days" given to the redactor, and the whole verse thus divided among *three different writers?* Simply for these reasons: P could not be allowed to speak of these forty days, because it would not be in agreement with his *presupposed* chronology. And they could not be given to J here, to whom they would naturally belong, since the statement in connection with which it is found ("the flood came on the earth"), would show that J knew of P's cause for producing the flood (the breaking in of the sea). Hence, these wholly unscientific manœuvres, *four radical changes being made in the text on this one subject of the chronology, within the limits of two chapters*. It is claimed, again, that it is P, the Elohist document, which represents the ark as having a door; but you will observe in 7: 16, that it is Jehovah who shuts the door upon the Patriarch. It is claimed that, according to P, the animals went into the ark by twos, male and female, while according to J they went in by sevens, clean animals; but noting 7: 3 and 7: 9 one will perceive that J knows and speaks of both sorts, and can only be made ignorant of them through two changes by the redactor.

It is particularly in the matter of language and style that resort is taken to this illogical and dangerous means of text-mutilation. There are certain stylistic peculiarities of one or the other document, it is claimed, which are fixed from the usage of previous chapters. But unfortunately for the scheme, they appear not infrequently in the wrong place. For instance, the expression "male and female" is held to be characteristic of P, J using another for it. In 7: 3 and 9, J uses this expression twice, and our critics must make the redactor deny it. The oft-recurring formula, "both man, beast, and creeping thing and fowl of the air" is found in the first chapter of Genesis and so is said to be characteristic of P. Here J has it in 6: 7 and 7: 23, and the redactor is called in to square the document to the theory. In 6: 7 there is still another fact not shown by the type. A Hebrew word meaning *create*, characteristic of P, is used in J. Why is it left unnoticed ? Apparently because it is thought that the redactor has already been given all the responsibility he can bear in a single verse.[1]

In all these changes, we are supposed to have the work of a redactor. How is it possible ? What motive could a redactor have had for it ? It is claimed by our critics that he has left the principal points of contrast between the two great documents from which he compiled in their original ruggedness. The principal changes made, with rare exceptions, are of single words, detached phrases, verses or parts of verses — every one of them changes in what was originally homogeneous matter to what is now heterogeneous, *from what was once true, from the point of view of the document, to what is now false*. There must have been some motive on his part. We fail to find an adequate, or a fairly rational one. The theory is, that a fabric of wool has been openly attached to one of cotton, or linen. The contrasted material, it is said, is evident enough, and even the very line of junction. The person who joined them together

---

[1] The same thing is true of this word in 2: 1b.

had no special reason, it is declared, to conceal the fact of composite material; indeed, he could not from really discerning eyes. Still, he has taken out here and there a fragment of one, and inserted it plumply in the midst of the other. *Why* has he done it? Suppose that one have before him the material for a statue or a bust. Part of it, the nucleus, we will say, which is stone, has been already shaped in rough outline, and is to be used as it is, unchanged. Another part, one-sixth, we will suppose (a fair proportion for the redactor's matter here), is plastic material, clay or plaster, which yields readily to the touch and can be easily manipulated. Which of the two parts is it that most conditions the problem and determines the result; the unchangeable nucleus or the plastic clay? Obviously the latter. It may be made to transform and completely misrepresent the other, whatever its original shape. Grant to our critics their extraordinary premises, and they will not trouble us for a conclusion; it is inevitable.

But we are not dependent here on counter literary criticism and evidence in rebuttal alone. We may also appeal directly to contemporaneous records. There was another story of the flood preserved in ancient Akkadia. Nearly 700 years B. C. there reigned in Nineveh a monarch by the name of Ashurbanipal. He was the grandson of the Biblical Sennacherib. Being a man of literary tastes, as well as a warrior, he enriched his capital with treasures of art and large collections of ancient documents. Among the latter was a copy of a famous epic, containing in the 11th of its twelve cantos, a full account of the flood, as current among the ancient Akkadians. This copy, Ashurbanipal's scribes transferred to tablets of clay directly from their originals, and subsequently, they were deposited in the vaults of the royal library at Nineveh. The date of the originals, it is generally admitted, cannot be far from that of Abraham, or about 2000 B. C. A few years ago these invaluable tablets, among many others, were transported to England. At that time none had more than the vaguest notion of their contents. In 1872, however, they were deciphered. To-day there is not the slightest doubt among scholars, that they furnish, from a polytheistic point of view, a duplicate narrative of the flood of Genesis, chaps. 6-9. Throughout, they follow the same general order of topics and their similarity in other respects is remarkable.

They agree, in the main, as it respects the region of the cataclysm; definitely in stating that the warning of it was first given to one man; that it was to be a flood; that it was on account of sin. This one man is bidden to prepare a vessel, whose dimensions and other details are stated; and he does as he is bidden. The object of the vessel is said to be to save the Akkadian Noah, and others, in order to "preserve the seed of life." The flood has *a second announcement* as in the Bible. The hero embarks with relatives and the beasts of the field. The door of the vessel is shut, and the flood appears as announced. It is caused by rain *and* the convulsions of nature. Mankind is destroyed. The duration of the flood is given. This other Noah, like the Biblical, opens a window. The ship strands in Armenia. Birds are sent out after seven days. The occupants of the ship disembark; a sacrifice is offered to the gods, who are pleased with the odor; and (as the text is generally read), a rainbow appears in the sky, and a promise is made that the world shall not again be so destroyed. At the end, the man and his wife are blessed by Bel. We have given the events in the order they are recorded in the Akkadian account.

Without entering into details, which are here impracticable, it is clear that the bearing of this account on the unity of the Biblical is direct. After a careful examination, we are unable to see why it is not *prima facie*, and really conclusive, evidence against the position of our critics. The Babylonian tablets contain, in the form of a continuous narrative, the more prominent facts of both the alleged Elohistic and Jevohistic sections of Genesis, and presents them mainly in the Biblical order, as one can plainly see. That is to say, several hundred years before the era of Moses, the principal contents of the Biblical narrative of the flood were current in ancient Akkadia, the general region from which, and at about the time when, Abraham set out, at God's command, to find a home in Canaan. How improbable, then, on its face, the theory that in Genesis we have two essentially different and discordant accounts, originating hundreds of years apart and united together at the period of the exile, B. C. 444! Our critics have made but a feeble effort to meet this argument. It is to be said, that, in general, they look askance at the testimony of the monuments. They do, however, say that while the cuneiform account of the flood largely agrees with the Biblical, it is only when the text is separated into its two documents as they would separate it. With the best will, and after a careful search, we fail to find one particular in which the Babylonian story differs from the combined accounts where it does not differ to the same extent precisely from the individual accounts. If it be meant, and this is probably what is meant, that the Akkadian account fails to harmonize discrepancies in the Biblical narrative found after it is divided by our critics, then we have another case of "begging the question." The discrepancies, as we have seen, are simply the fruit of the division.

It is enough for present purposes, that this highly providential and universally accredited witness, speaking to us from the home and the age of the patriarch Abraham, testifies: (1), to the contemporaneousness, then and there, of the alleged two accounts of the deluge found in the Bible; and (2), to the fact that, at that time and place, they were found already combined in one account as they are now, and as far as we know, have always been. The subordinate matter, whether the Bible narrative antedates the Akkadian, and their mutual relations in other respects, depend, largely on one's point of view. He who believes that God revealed himself to primitive man as one God, as the Bible tells us, will be likely to see in the Akkadian story a polytheistic corruption of an original monotheistic account, and as such, strongly confirmatory of the historicity of Genesis.

Such now, in brief survey, is the kind of reasoning adopted by the advocates of the common theory of Pentateuchal analysis; and in some such way as we have suggested, it may be fairly tested. It would have been far more congenial to the present writer to engage in Biblical studies more apparently practical, and more directly constructive. But he had no option, nor has any other conscientious student, while this obtrusive theory holds the field. He must be loyal to the motto of our title-page. It is no less scientific, than it is Biblical, in its spirit. Besides, in the end, could anything be more truly practical or constructive, than to proceed to find out, by word for word examination, whether the scheme of Pentateuchal analysis now in vogue can be scientifically defended? This very method, if faithfully pursued, will result in something more than negative conclusions. It reaches far beyond the limits which our critics have set for themselves. It will, in fact, determine as far as any literary criticism can, whether any other theory of the origin and composition of the Pentateuch needs to be substituted for the so-called traditional one. And if it shall appear, as to us seems probable, that not only were original sources used in the composition of Genesis, but that their limits, with some degree of probability, may be pointed out, the result will be neither singular nor unwelcome. In the meantime, let the freest and fullest criticism of the Scriptures, high and low, be encouraged so far as it is serious, inductive not only in name but in fact, and thoroughly fair.

The present crying need has been well expressed by Professor Robertson: "It is of a criticism that shall start by admitting that the writer possessed ordinary intelligence, and knows fairly well what he is writing about; that shall then interpret his words in a fair and common-sense fashion, and be bold enough, when necessary, to confess its own ignorance. . . The critical theory is fast becoming 'traditional,' and is being accepted by multitudes on no better grounds than those on which the former view became traditional. It is now high time to apply skepticism to the prevailing theory, so that the strength or weakness of its foundations may be made manifest."[1]

HARTFORD, in May, 1892.

[1] *Ibid.*, p. viii.

GENESIS IN COLORS.

EXPLANATION OF COLORS, Etc.

Matter in this color belongs to P.

Matter in this color belongs to J.

Matter in this color belongs to the Redactor.

Matter in this color belongs to J².

Matter in this color belongs to JE.

Matter in this color belongs to E.

<u>Matter thus underlined represents a gloss.</u>

In order to know from the English when the word *Elohim* and *Jehovah* are found in the Hebrew, attention should be given to the foot-notes as on pp. 2, 14, *etc.*, as also to the rules adopted by the Revisers and printed in the Preface to the Revised edition of the English Bible.

THE FIRST BOOK OF MOSES, COMMONLY CALLED

GENESIS.

1 In the beginning God created the heaven and the earth. (2) And the earth was waste and void; and darkness was upon the face of the deep: and the spirit of God [1] moved upon the face of the waters. (3) And God said, Let there be light: and there was light. (4) And God saw the light, that it was good: and God divided the light from the darkness. (5) And God called the light Day, and the darkness he called Night. And there was evening and there was morning, one day.

(6) And God said, Let there be a [2] firmament in the midst of the waters, and let it divide the waters from the waters. (7) And God made the firmament, and divided the waters which were under the firmament from the waters which were above the firmament: and it was so. (8) And God called the firmament Heaven. And there was evening and there was morning, a second day.

(9) And God said, Let the waters under the heaven be gathered together unto one place, and let the dry land appear: and it was so. (10) And God called the dry land Earth; and the gathering together of the waters called he Seas: and God saw that it was good. (11) And God said, Let the earth put forth grass, herb yielding seed, *and* fruit tree bearing fruit after its kind, wherein is the seed thereof, upon the earth: and it was so. (12) And the earth brought forth grass, herb yielding seed after its kind, and tree bearing fruit, wherein is the seed thereof, after its kind: and God saw that it was good. (13) And there was evening and there was morning, a third day.

(14) And God said, Let there be lights in the firmament of the heaven to divide the day from the night; and let them be for signs, and for seasons, and for days and years: (15) and let them be for lights in the firmament of the heaven to give light upon the earth: and it was so. (16) And God made the two great lights; the greater light to rule the day, and the lesser light to rule the night: *he made* the stars also. (17) And God set them in the firmament of the heaven to give light upon the earth, (18) and to rule over the day and over the night, and to divide the light from the darkness: and God saw that it was good. (19) And there was evening and there was morning, a fourth day.

(20) And God said, Let the waters [3] bring forth abundantly the moving creature that hath life, and let fowl fly above the earth [4] in the open firmament of heaven. (21) And God created the great sea-monsters, and every living creature that moveth, which the waters brought forth abundantly, after their kinds, and every winged fowl after its kind: and God saw that it was good. (22) And God blessed

---

[1] Or, *was brooding upon*. [2] Heb. *expanse*. [3] Heb. *swarm with swarms of living creatures*. [4] Heb. *on the face of the expanse of the heaven*.

1

them, saying, Be fruitful, and multiply, and fill the waters in the seas, and let fowl multiply in the earth. (23) And there was evening and there was morning, a fifth day.

(24) And God said, Let the earth bring forth the living creature after its kind, cattle, and creeping thing, and beast of the earth after its kind: and it was so. (25) And God made the beast of the earth after its kind, and the cattle after their kind, and every thing that creepeth upon the ground after its kind: and God saw that it was good. (26) And God said, Let us make man in our image, after our likeness: and let them have dominion over the fish of the sea, and over the fowl of the air, and over the cattle, and over all the earth, and over every creeping thing that creepeth upon the earth. (27) And God created man in his own image, in the image of God created he him; male and female created he them. (28) And God blessed them: and God said unto them, Be fruitful, and multiply, and replenish the earth, and subdue it: and have dominion over the fish of the sea, and over the fowl of the air, and over every living thing that ¹moveth upon the earth. (29) And God said, Behold, I have given you every herb yielding seed, which is upon the face of all the earth, and every tree, in the which is the fruit of a tree yielding seed; to you it shall be for meat: (30) and to every beast of the earth, and to every fowl of the air, and to every thing that creepeth upon the earth, wherein there is ²life, *I have given* every green herb for meat: and it was so. (31) And God saw every thing that he had made, and, behold, it was very good. And there was evening and there was morning, the sixth day.

2 And the heaven and the earth were finished, and all the host of them. (2) And on the seventh day God finished his work which he had made: and he rested on the seventh day from all his work which he had made. (3) And God blessed the seventh day, and hallowed it: because that in it he rested from all his work which God had created and made.

(4) These are the generations of the heaven and of the earth when they were created, in the day that ³the LORD God made earth and heaven. (5) And no plant of the field was yet in the earth, and no herb of the field had yet sprung up: for the LORD God had not caused it to rain upon the earth, and there was not a man to till the ground; (6) but there went up a mist from the earth, and watered the whole face of the ground. (7) And the LORD God formed man of the dust of the ground, and breathed into his nostrils the breath of life; and man became a living soul. (8) And the LORD God planted a garden eastward, in Eden; and there he put the man whom he had formed. (9) And out of the ground made the LORD God to grow every tree that is pleasant to the sight, and good for food; the tree of life also in the midst of the garden, and the tree of the knowledge of good and evil. (10) And a river went out of Eden to water the garden; and from thence it was parted, and became four heads. (11) The name of the first is Pishon: that is it which compasseth the whole land of Havilah, where there is gold; (12) and the gold of that land is good: there is bdellium and the ⁴onyx stone. (13) And the name of the second river is Gihon: the same is it that compasseth the whole land of Cush. And the name of the third river is Hiddekel: that is it which goeth ⁶toward the east of Assyria. And the fourth river is Euphrates. (15) And the LORD God took the man, and put him into the garden of Eden to dress it and to keep it. (16) And the

---

¹ Or, *creepeth*. ² Heb. *a living soul*. ³ Heb *Jehovah*, as in other places where LORD is put in capitals. ⁴ Or, *beryl*. ⁵ That is, *Tigris*. ⁶ Or, *toward the east of*.

LORD God commanded the man, saying, Of every tree of the garden thou mayest freely eat: (17) but of the tree of the knowledge of good and evil, thou shalt not eat of it: for in the day that thou eatest thereof thou shalt surely die.

(18) And the LORD God said, It is not good that the man should be alone; I will make him an help ¹ meet for him. (19) And out of the ground the LORD God formed every beast of the field, and every fowl of the air; and brought them unto the man to see what he would call them: and whatsoever the man called every living creature, that was the name thereof. (20) And the man gave names to all cattle, and to the fowl of the air, and to every beast of the field; but for ² man there was not found an help meet for him. (21) And the LORD God caused a deep sleep to fall upon the man, and he slept; and he took one of his ribs, and closed up the flesh instead thereof: (22) and the rib, which the LORD God had taken from the man, ³ made he a woman, and brought her unto the man. (23) And the man said, This is now bone of my bones, and flesh of my flesh: she shall be called ⁴ Woman, because she was taken out of ⁵ Man. (24) Therefore shall a man leave his father and his mother, and shall cleave unto his wife: and they shall be one flesh. (25) And they were both naked, the man and his wife, and were not ashamed.

3 Now the serpent was more subtil than any beast of the field which the LORD God had made. And he said unto the woman, Yea, hath God said, Ye shall not eat of ⁶ any tree of the garden? (2) And the woman said unto the serpent, Of the fruit of the trees of the garden we may eat: (3) but of the fruit of the tree which is in the midst of the garden, God hath said, Ye shall not eat of it, neither shall ye touch it, lest ye die. (4) And the serpent said unto the woman, Ye shall not surely die: (5) for God doth know that in the day ye eat thereof, then your eyes shall be opened, and ye shall be as ⁷ God, knowing good and evil. (6) And when the woman saw that the tree was good for food, and that it was a delight to the eyes, and that the tree was ⁸ to be desired to make one wise, she took of the fruit thereof, and did eat; and she gave also unto her husband with her, and he did eat. (7) And the eyes of them both were opened, and they knew that they were naked; and they sewed fig leaves together, and made themselves ⁹ aprons. (8) And they heard the ¹⁰ voice of the LORD God walking in the garden in the ¹¹ cool of the day: and the man and his wife hid themselves from the presence of the LORD God amongst the trees of the garden. (9) And the LORD God called unto the man, and said unto him, Where art thou? (10) And he said, I heard thy ¹⁰ voice in the garden, and I was afraid, because I was naked; and I hid myself. (11) And he said, Who told thee that thou wast naked? Hast thou eaten of the tree, whereof I commanded thee that thou shouldest not eat? (12) And the man said, The woman whom thou gavest to be with me, she gave me of the tree, and I did eat. (13) And the LORD God said unto the woman, What is this thou hast done? And the woman said, The serpent beguiled me, and I did eat. (14) And the LORD God said unto the serpent, Because thou hast done this, cursed art thou ¹² above all cattle, and ¹² above every beast of the field; upon thy belly shalt thou go, and dust shalt thou eat all the days of thy life: (15) and I will put enmity between thee and the woman, and between thy seed and her seed: it shall ¹³ bruise thy head, and thou shalt ¹³ bruise his heel. (16) Unto the woman he said, I will greatly multiply thy sorrow and thy

---

¹ Or, *answering to.* ² Or, *Adam.* ³ Heb. *builded he into.* ⁴ Heb. *Isshah.* ⁵ Heb. *Ish.* ⁶ Or, *all the trees.* ⁷ Or, *gods.* ⁸ Or, *desirable to look upon.* ⁹ Or, *girdles.* ¹⁰ Or, *sound.* ¹¹ Heb. *wind.* ¹² Or, *from among.* ¹³ Or, *lie in wait for.*

conception; in sorrow thou shalt bring forth children; and thy desire shall be to thy husband, and he shall rule over thee. (17) And unto Adam he said, Because thou hast hearkened unto the voice of thy wife, and hast eaten of the tree, of which I commanded thee, saying, Thou shalt not eat of it: cursed is the ground for thy sake; in ¹toil shalt thou eat of it all the days of thy life; (18) thorns also and thistles shall it bring forth to thee; and thou shalt eat the herb of the field; (19) in the sweat of thy face shalt thou eat bread, till thou return unto the ground: for out of it wast thou taken: for dust thou art, and unto dust shalt thou return. (20) And the man called his wife's name ²Eve; because she was the mother of all living. (21) And the LORD God made for Adam and for his wife coats of skins, and clothed them.

(22) And the LORD God said, Behold, the man is become as one of us, to know good and evil; and now, lest he put forth his hand, and take also of the tree of life, and eat, and live for ever: (23) therefore the LORD God sent him forth from the garden of Eden, to till the ground from whence he was taken. (24) So he drove out the man; and he placed at the east of the garden of Eden the Cherubim, and the flame of a sword which turned every way, to keep the way of the tree of life.

4 And the man knew Eve his wife; and she conceived, and bare Cain, and said, I have ³gotten a man with *the help of* the LORD. (2) And again she bare his brother Abel. And Abel was a keeper of sheep, but Cain was a tiller of the ground. (3) And in process of time it came to pass, that Cain brought of the fruit of the ground an offering unto the LORD. (4) And Abel, he also brought of the firstlings of his flock and of the fat thereof. And the LORD had respect unto Abel and to his offering: (5) but unto Cain and to his offering he had not respect. And Cain was very wroth, and his countenance fell. (6) And the LORD said unto Cain, Why art thou wroth? and why is thy countenance fallen? (7) If thou doest well, ⁴shalt thou not be accepted? and if thou doest not well, sin coucheth at the door: and unto thee ⁵shall be his desire, and thou shalt rule over him. (8) And Cain ⁶told Abel his brother. And it came to pass, when they were in the field, that Cain rose up against Abel his brother, and slew him. (9) And the LORD said unto Cain, Where is Abel thy brother? And he said, I know not: am I my brother's keeper? (10) And he said, What hast thou done? the voice of thy brother's blood crieth unto me from the ground. (11) And now cursed art thou from the ground, which hath opened her mouth to receive thy brother's blood from thy hand; (12) when thou tillest the ground, it shall not henceforth yield unto thee her strength; a fugitive and a wanderer shalt thou be in the earth. (13) And Cain said unto the LORD, ⁷My punishment is greater ⁸than I can bear. (14) Behold, thou hast driven me out this day from the face of the ground; and from thy face shall I be hid; and I shall be a fugitive and a wanderer in the earth; and it shall come to pass, that whosoever findeth me shall slay me. (15) And the LORD said unto him, Therefore whosoever slayeth Cain, vengeance shall be taken on him sevenfold. And the LORD appointed a sign for Cain, lest any finding him should smite him.

(16) And Cain went out from the presence of the LORD, and dwelt in the land of Nod, on the east of Eden. (17) And ... his ...

---

¹ Or, *sorrow*. ² Heb. *Havvah*, that is, *Living*, or, *Life*. ³ Heb. *kanah*, to get. ⁴ Or, *shall it not be lifted up?* ⁵ Or, *is its desire, but thou shouldest rule over it.* ⁶ Heb. *said unto*. Many ancient authorities have, *said unto Abel his brother, Let us go into the field.* ⁷ Or, *Mine iniquity.* ⁸ Or, *than can be forgiven.* ⁹ That is, *Wandering.* ¹⁰ Or, *in front of.*

GENESIS. 5

a city, and called the name of the city, after the name of his son, Enoch. (18) And unto Enoch was born Irad: and Irad begat Mehujael: and Mehujael begat Methushael: and Methushael begat Lamech. (19) And Lamech took unto him two wives: the name of the one was Adah, and the name of the other Zillah. (20) And Adah bare Jabal: he was the father of such as dwell in tents and *have* cattle. (21) And his brother's name was Jubal: he was the father of all such as handle the harp and pipe. (22) And Zillah, she also bare Tubal-cain, ¹the forger of every cutting instrument of ²brass and iron: and the sister of Tubal-cain was Naamah. (23) And Lamech said unto his wives:

Adah and Zillah, hear my voice;
Ye wives of Lamech, hearken unto my speech:
For ³I have slain a man ⁴for wounding me,
And a young man for bruising me:
(24) If Cain shall be avenged sevenfold,
Truly Lamech seventy and sevenfold.

(25) **And Adam knew his wife again; and she bare a son, and called his name** ⁵**Seth: For,** *said she,* **God** ⁶**hath appointed me another seed instead of Abel; for Cain slew him.** (26) **And to Seth, to him also there was born a son; and he called his name Enosh: then began men to call upon the name of the LORD.**

5 This is the book of the generations of Adam. In the day that God created man, in the likeness of God made he him; (2) male and female created he them; and blessed them, and called their name ⁷Adam, in the day when they were created. (3) And Adam lived an hundred and thirty years, and begat *a son* in his own likeness, after his image; and called his name Seth: (4) and the days of Adam after he begat Seth were eight hundred years: and he begat sons and daughters. (5) And all the days that Adam lived were nine hundred and thirty years: and he died.

(6) And Seth lived an hundred and five years, and begat Enosh: (7) and Seth lived after he begat Enosh eight hundred and seven years, and begat sons and daughters: (8) and all the days of Seth were nine hundred and twelve years: and he died.

(9) And Enosh lived ninety years, and begat Kenan: (10) and Enosh lived after he begat Kenan eight hundred and fifteen years, and begat sons and daughters: (11) and all the days of Enosh were nine hundred and five years: and he died.

(12) And Kenan lived seventy years, and begat Mahalalel: (13) and Kenan lived after he begat Mahalalel eight hundred and forty years, and begat sons and daughters: (14) and all the days of Kenan were nine hundred and ten years: and he died.

(15) And Mahalalel lived sixty and five years, and begat Jared: (16) and Mahalalel lived after he begat Jared eight hundred and thirty years, and begat sons and daughters: (17) and all the days of Mahalalel were eight hundred ninety and five years: and he died.

(18) And Jared lived an hundred sixty and two years, and begat Enoch: (19) and Jared lived after he begat Enoch eight hundred years, and begat sons and daughters: (20) and all the days of Jared were nine hundred sixty and two years: and he died.

(21) And Enoch lived sixty and five years, and begat Methuselah: (22) and Enoch walked with God after he begat Methuselah three hundred years, and begat sons and daughters: (23) and all the days of Enoch were three hundred sixty and five years: (24) and Enoch walked

---

¹ Or, *an instructor of every artificer.* ² Or, copper, and so elsewhere. ³ Or, *I will slay.* ⁴ Or, *to my wounding, and a young man to my hurt.* ⁵ Heb. *Sheth.* ⁶ Heb. *shath.* ⁷ Or, *Man.*

with God: and he was not; for God took him.

(25) And Methuselah lived an hundred eighty and seven years, and begat Lamech: (26) and Methuselah lived after he begat Lamech seven hundred eighty and two years, and begat sons and daughters: (27) and all the days of Methuselah were nine hundred sixty and nine years: and he died.

(28) And Lamech lived an hundred eighty and two years, and begat a son: (29) and he called his name Noah, saying, This same shall [1] comfort us for our work and for the toil of our hands, [2] because of the ground which the LORD hath cursed. (30) And Lamech lived after he begat Noah five hundred ninety and five years, and begat sons and daughters: (31) and all the days of Lamech were seven hundred seventy and seven years: and he died.

(32) And Noah was five hundred years old: and Noah begat Shem, Ham, and Japheth.

(**6** And it came to pass, when men began to multiply on the face of the ground, and daughters were born unto them, (2) that the sons of God saw the daughters of men that they were fair: and they took them wives of all that they chose. (3) And the LORD said, My spirit shall not [a] strive with man for ever, [4] for that he also is flesh: [5] yet shall his days be an hundred and twenty years. (4) The [6] Nephilim were in the earth in those days, and also after that, when the sons of God came in unto the daughters of men, and they bare children to them: the same were the mighty men which were of old, the men of renown. (5) And the LORD saw that the wickedness of man was great in the earth, and that every imagination of the thoughts of his heart was only evil continually. (6) And it repented the LORD that he had made man on the earth, and it grieved him at his heart. (7) And the LORD said, I will [7] destroy man whom I have created from the face of the ground; both man, and beast, and creeping thing, and fowl of the air; for it repenteth me that I have made them. (8) But Noah found grace in the eyes of the LORD.

(9) These are the generations of Noah. Noah was a righteous man, and [8] perfect in his generations: Noah walked with God. (10) And Noah begat three sons, Shem, Ham, and Japheth. (11) And the earth was corrupt before God, and the earth was filled with violence. (12) And God saw the earth, and, behold, it was corrupt: for all flesh had corrupted his way upon the earth.

(13) And God said unto Noah, The end of all flesh is come before me; for the earth is filled with violence through them; and, behold, I will destroy them with the earth. (14) Make thee an ark of gopher wood; [9] rooms shalt thou make in the ark, and shalt pitch it within and without with pitch. (15) And this is how thou shalt make it: the length of the ark three hundred cubits, the breadth of it fifty cubits, and the height of it thirty cubits. (16) A [10] light shalt thou make to the ark, and to a cubit shalt thou finish it [11] upward; and the door of the ark shalt thou set in the side thereof; with lower, second, and third stories shalt thou make it. (17) And I, behold, I do bring the flood of waters upon the earth, to destroy all flesh, wherein is the breath of life, from under heaven; every thing that is in the earth shall die. (18) But I will establish my covenant with thee: and thou shalt come into the ark, thou, and thy sons, and thy wife, and thy sons' wives with thee. (19) And of every living thing of all flesh, two of every sort shalt thou bring into the ark,

---

[1] Heb. *naḥem*, to comfort. [2] Or, which cometh *from the ground*. [3] Or, *rule in*. Or, according to many ancient versions, *abide in*. [4] Or, *in their going astray they are flesh*. [5] Or, *therefore*. [6] Or, *giants*. See Num. xiii. 33. [7] Heb. *blot out*. [8] Or, *blameless*. [9] Heb. *nests*. [10] Or, *roof*. [11] Or, *from above*.

to keep them alive with thee; they shall be male and female. (20) Of the fowl after their kind, and of the cattle after their kind, of every creeping thing of the ground after its kind, two of every sort shall come unto thee, to keep them alive. (21) And take thou unto thee of all food that is eaten, and gather it to thee; and it shall be for food for thee, and for them. (22) Thus did Noah; according to all that God commanded him, so did he.

7 And the LORD said unto Noah, Come thou and all thy house into the ark; for thee have I seen righteous before me in this generation. (2) Of every clean beast thou shalt take to thee seven and seven, the male and his female; and of the beasts that are not clean two, the male and his female; (3) of the fowl also of the air, seven and seven, male and female: to keep seed alive upon the face of all the earth. (4) For yet seven days, and I will cause it to rain upon the earth forty days and forty nights; and every living thing that I have made will I [1]destroy from off the face of the ground. (5) And Noah did according unto all that the LORD commanded him.

(6) And Noah was six hundred years old when the flood of waters was upon the earth. (7) And Noah went in, and his sons, and his wife, and his sons' wives with him, into the ark, because of the waters of the flood. (8) Of clean beasts, and of beasts that are not clean, and of fowls, and of every thing that creepeth upon the ground, (9) there went in two and two unto Noah into the ark, male and female, as God commanded Noah. (10) And it came to pass after the seven days, that the waters of the flood were upon the earth. (11) In the six hundredth year of Noah's life, in the second month, on the seventeenth day of the month, on the same day were all the fountains of the great deep broken up, and the windows of heaven were opened. (12) And the rain was upon the earth forty days and forty nights. (13) In the selfsame day entered Noah, and Shem, and Ham, and Japheth, the sons of Noah, and Noah's wife, and the three wives of his sons with them, into the ark; (14) they, and every beast after its kind, and all the cattle after their kind, and every creeping thing that creepeth upon the earth after its kind, and every fowl after its kind, every bird of every [2]sort. (15) And they went in unto Noah into the ark, two and two of all flesh wherein is the breath of life. (16) And they that went in, went in male and female of all flesh, as God commanded him: and the LORD shut him in. (17) And the flood was forty days upon the earth; and the waters increased, and bare up the ark, and it was lift up above the earth. (18) And the waters prevailed, and increased greatly upon the earth; and the ark went upon the face of the waters. (19) And the waters prevailed exceedingly upon the earth; and all the high mountains that were under the whole heaven were covered. (20) Fifteen cubits upward did the waters prevail; and the mountains were covered. (21) And all flesh died that moved upon the earth, both fowl, and cattle, and beast, and every [3]creeping thing that creepeth upon the earth, and every man: (22) all in whose nostrils was the breath of the spirit of life, of all that was in the dry land, died. (23) [4]And every living thing was [5]destroyed which was upon the face of the ground, both man, and cattle, and creeping thing, and fowl of the heaven; and they were destroyed from the earth: and Noah only was left, and they that were with him in the ark. (24) And the waters prevailed upon the earth an hundred and fifty days.

---

[1] Heb. *blot out.*   [2] Heb. *wing.*   [3] Or, *swarming thing that swarmeth.*   [4] Or, *And he destroyed every living thing.*   [5] Heb. *blotted out.*

8 And God remembered Noah, and every living thing, and all the cattle that were with him in the ark: and God made a wind to pass over the earth, and the waters assuaged; (2) the fountains also of the deep and the windows of heaven were stopped, **and the rain from heaven was restrained**; (3) **and the waters returned from off the earth continually**: and after the end of an hundred and fifty days the waters decreased. (4) And the ark rested in the seventh month, on the seventeenth day of the month, upon the mountains of Ararat. (5) And the waters decreased continually until the tenth month: in the tenth month, on the first day of the month, were the tops of the mountains seen. (6) And it came to pass at the end of forty days, that Noah opened the window of the ark which he had made: (7) and he sent forth a raven, and it went forth to and fro, until the waters were dried up from off the earth. (8) And he sent forth a dove from him, to see if the waters were abated from off the face of the ground; (9) but the dove found no rest for the sole of her foot, and she returned unto him to the ark, for the waters were on the face of the whole earth: and he put forth his hand, and took her, and brought her in unto him into the ark. (10) And he stayed yet other seven days; and again he sent forth the dove out of the ark; (11) and the dove came in to him at eventide; and, lo, in her mouth [1] an olive leaf pluckt off: so Noah knew that the waters were abated from off the earth. (12) And he stayed yet other seven days; and sent forth the dove; and she returned not again unto him any more. (13) And it came to pass in the six hundred and first year, in the first month, the first day of the month, the waters were dried up from off the earth: **and Noah removed the covering of the ark, and looked, and, behold, the face of the ground was dried.**

(14) And in the second month, on the seven and twentieth day of the month, was the earth dry.

(15) And God spake unto Noah, saying, (16) Go forth of the ark, thou, and thy wife, and thy sons, and thy sons' wives with thee. (17) Bring forth with thee every living thing that is with thee of all flesh, both fowl, and cattle, and every creeping thing that creepeth upon the earth; that they may breed abundantly in the earth, and be fruitful, and multiply upon the earth. (18) And Noah went forth, and his sons, and his wife, and his sons' wives with him: (19) every beast, every creeping thing, and every fowl, whatsoever moveth upon the earth, after their families, went forth out of the ark. (20) And Noah builded an altar unto the LORD; and took of every clean beast, and of every clean fowl, and offered burnt offerings on the altar. (21) And the LORD smelled the sweet savour; and the LORD said in his heart, I will not again curse the ground any more for man's [2] sake, for that the imagination of man's heart is evil from his youth; neither will I again smite any more every thing living, as I have done. (22) While the earth remaineth, seedtime and harvest, and cold and heat, and summer and winter, and day and night shall not cease. **9** And God blessed Noah and his sons, and said unto them, Be fruitful, and multiply, and replenish the earth. (2) And the fear of you and the dread of you shall be upon every beast of the earth, and upon every fowl of the air: with all wherewith the ground [3] teemeth, and all the fishes of the sea, into your hand are they delivered. (3) Every moving thing that liveth shall be food for you: as the green herb have I given you all. (4) But flesh with the life thereof, *which is* the blood thereof, shall ye not eat. (5) And surely your blood, *the blood* of your lives, will I require; at the hand

---

[1] Or, *a fresh olive leaf.*   [2] Or, *sake; for the.*   [3] Or, *creepeth.*

of every beast will I require it: and at the hand of man, even at the hand of every man's brother, will I require the life of man. (6) Whoso sheddeth man's blood, by man shall his blood be shed: for in the image of God made he man. (7) And you, be ye fruitful, and multiply; bring forth abundantly in the earth, and multiply therein.

(8) And God spake unto Noah, and to his sons with him, saying, (9) And I, behold, I establish my covenant with you, and with your seed after you; (10) and with every living creature that is with you, the fowl, the cattle, and every beast of the earth with you; of all that go out of the ark, even every beast of the earth. (11) And I will establish my covenant with you; neither shall all flesh be cut off any more by the waters of the flood; neither shall there any more be a flood to destroy the earth. (12) And God said, This is the token of the covenant which I make between me and you and every living creature that is with you, for perpetual generations: (13) ¹I do set my bow in the cloud, and it shall be for a token of a covenant between me and the earth. (14) And it shall come to pass, when I bring a cloud over the earth, that the bow shall be seen in the cloud, (15) and I will remember my covenant, which is between me and you and every living creature of all flesh; and the waters shall no more become a flood to destroy all flesh. (16) And the bow shall be in the cloud; and I will look upon it, that I may remember the everlasting covenant between God and every living creature of all flesh that is upon the earth. (17) And God said unto Noah, This is the token of the covenant which I have established between me and all flesh that is upon the earth.

(18) And the sons of Noah, that went forth of the ark, were Shem, and Ham, and Japheth: and Ham is the father of Canaan. (19) These three were the sons of Noah: and of these was the whole earth overspread.

(20) And Noah began to be an husbandman, and planted a vineyard: (21) and he drank of the wine, and was drunken; and he was uncovered within his tent. (22) And Ham, the father of Canaan, saw the nakedness of his father, and told his two brethren without. (23) And Shem and Japheth took a garment, and laid it upon both their shoulders, and went backward, and covered the nakedness of their father; and their faces were backward, and they saw not their father's nakedness. (24) And Noah awoke from his wine, and knew what his ²youngest son had done unto him. (25) And he said,

Cursed be Canaan;
A servant of servants shall he be unto his brethren.

(26) And he said,

Blessed be the LORD, the God of Shem;
And let Canaan be ³his servant.
(27) God enlarge Japheth,
And ⁴let him dwell in the tents of Shem;
And let Canaan be ³his servant.

(28) And Noah lived after the flood three hundred and fifty years. (29) And all the days of Noah were nine hundred and fifty years: and he died.

10 Now these are the generations of the sons of Noah, Shem Ham and Japheth: (and unto them were sons born after the flood.)

(2) The sons of Japheth: Gomer, and Magog, and Madai, and Javan, and Tubal, and Meshech, and Tiras. (3) And the sons of Gomer; Ashkenaz, and ⁵ Riphath, and Togarmah. (4) And the sons of Javan; Elishah, and Tarshish, Kittim, and ⁶ Dodanim. (5) Of these were the

---

¹ Or, *I have set.*   ² Or, *younger.*   ³ Or, *their.*   ⁴ Or, *he shall.*   ⁵ In 1 Chr. i. 6, *Diphath.*   ⁶ In 1 Chr. i. 7, *Rodanim.*

¹ isles of the nations divided in their lands, every one after his tongue; after their families, in their nations.

(6) And the sons of Ham; Cush, and Mizraim, and Put, and Canaan. (7) And the sons of Cush ; Seba, and Havilah, and Sabtah, and Raamah, and Sabteca: and the sons of Raamah ; Sheba, and Dedan. (8) And Cush begat Nimrod: he began to be a mighty one in the earth. (9) He was a mighty hunter before the LORD: wherefore it is said, Like Nimrod a mighty hunter before the LORD. (10) And the beginning of his kingdom was Babel, and Erech, and Accad, and Calneh, in the land of Shinar. (11) Out of that land ² he went forth into Assyria, and builded Nineveh, and Rehoboth-Ir, and Calah, (12) and Resen between Nineveh and Calah (the same is the great city). (13) And Mizraim begat Ludim, and Anamim, and Lehabim, and Naphtuhim, (14) and Pathrusim, and Casluhim (whence went forth ³ the Philistines), and Caphtorim.

(15) And Canaan begat Zidon his firstborn, and Heth ; (16) and the Jebusite, and the Amorite, and the Girgashite; (17) and the Hivite, and the Arkite, and the Sinite, (18) and the Arvadite, and the Zemarite, and the Hamathite: and afterward were the families of the Canaanite spread abroad. (19) And the border of the Canaanite was from Zidon, as thou goest toward Gerar, unto Gaza; as thou goest toward Sodom and Gomorrah and Admah and Zeboiim, unto Lasha. (20) These are the sons of Ham, after their families, after their tongues, in their lands, in their nations.

(21) And unto Shem, the father of all the children of Eber, ⁴ the elder brother of Japheth, to him also were children born. (22) The sons of Shem ; Elam, and Asshur, and Arpachshad, and Lud, and Aram. (23) And the sons of Aram ; Uz, and Hul, and Gether, and Mash. (24) And Arpachshad begat ⁵ Shelah; and Shelah begat Eber. (25) And unto Eber were born two sons : the name of the one was ⁶ Peleg ; for in his days was the earth divided ; and his brother's name was Joktan. (26) And Joktan begat Almodad, and Sheleph, and Hazarmaveth, and Jerah ; (27) and Hadoram, and Uzal, and Diklah ; (28) and ⁷ Obal, and Abimael, and Sheba ; (29) and Ophir, and Havilah, and Jobab : all these were the sons of Joktan. (30) And their dwelling was from Mesha, as thou goest toward Sephar, the ⁸ mountain of the east. (31) These are the sons of Shem, after their families, after their tongues, in their lands, after their nations.

(32) These are the families of the sons of Noah, after their generations, in their nations : and of these were the nations divided in the earth after the flood.

11 And the whole earth was of one ⁹ language and of one ¹⁰ speech. (2) And it came to pass, as they journeyed ¹¹ east, that they found a plain in the land of Shinar; and they dwelt there. (3) And they said one to another, Go to, let us make brick, and burn them thoroughly. And they had brick for stone, and ¹² slime had they for mortar. (4) And they said, Go to, let us build us a city, and a tower, whose top may reach unto heaven; and let us make us a name, lest we be scattered abroad upon the face of the whole earth. (5) And the LORD came down to see the city and the tower, which the children of men builded. (6) And the LORD said, Behold, they are one people, and they have all one language; and this is what they begin to do: and now nothing will be withholden from them, which they purpose to do. (7) Go to, let us go down, and there confound their language, that they may not understand one another's

¹ Or, coast-lands. ² Or, went forth Asshur. ³ Heb. Pelishtim. ⁴ Or, the brother of Japheth the elder. ⁵ The Sept. reads, begat Cainan, and Cainan begat Shelah. ⁶ That is, Division. ⁷ In 1 Chr. i. 22, Ebal. ⁸ Or, hill country. ⁹ Heb. lip. ¹⁰ Heb. words. ¹¹ Or, in the east. ¹² That is, bitumen.

GENESIS. 11

speech. (8) So the LORD scattered them abroad from thence upon the face of all the earth: and they left off to build the city. (9) Therefore was the name of it called Babel; because the LORD did there [1] confound the language of all the earth: and from thence did the LORD scatter them abroad upon the face of all the earth.

(10) These are the generations of Shem. Shem was an hundred years old, and begat Arpachshad two years after the flood: (11) and Shem lived after he begat Arpachshad five hundred years, and begat sons and daughters.

(12) And Arpachshad lived five and thirty years, and begat Shelah: (13) and Arpachshad lived after he begat Shelah four hundred and three years, and begat sons and daughters.

(14) And Shelah lived thirty years, and begat Eber: (15) and Shelah lived after he begat Eber four hundred and three years, and begat sons and daughters.

(16) And Eber lived four and thirty years, and begat Peleg: (17) and Eber lived after he begat Peleg four hundred and thirty years, and begat sons and daughters.

(18) And Peleg lived thirty years, and begat Reu: (19) and Peleg lived after he begat Reu two hundred and nine years, and begat sons and daughters.

(20) And Reu lived two and thirty years, and begat Serug: (21) and Reu lived after he begat Serug two hundred and seven years, and begat sons and daughters.

(22) And Serug lived thirty years, and begat Nahor: (23) and Serug lived after he begat Nahor two hundred years, and begat sons and daughters.

(24) And Nahor lived nine and twenty years, and begat Terah: (25) and Nahor lived after he begat Terah an hundred and nineteen years, and begat sons and daughters.

(26) And Terah lived seventy years, and begat Abram, Nahor, and Haran.

(27) Now these are the generations of Terah. Terah begat Abram, Nahor, and Haran; and Haran begat Lot. (28) And Haran died in the presence of his father Terah in the land of his nativity, in Ur of the Chaldees. (29) And Abram and Nahor took them wives: the name of Abram's wife was Sarai; and the name of Nahor's wife, Milcah, the daughter of Haran, the father of Milcah, and the father of Iscah. (30) And Sarai was barren; she had no child. (31) And Terah took Abram his son, and Lot the son of Haran, his son's son, and Sarai his daughter in law, his son Abram's wife; and they went forth with them from Ur of the Chaldees, to go into the land of Canaan; and they came unto Haran, and dwelt there. (32) And the days of Terah were two hundred and five years: and Terah died in Haran.

12 Now the LORD said unto Abram, Get thee out of thy country, and from thy kindred, and from thy father's house, unto the land that I will shew thee: (2) and I will make of thee a great nation, and I will bless thee, and make thy name great; and be thou a blessing: (3) and I will bless them that bless thee, and him that curseth thee will I curse: and in thee shall all the families of the earth be blessed. (4) So Abram went, as the LORD had spoken unto him; and Lot went with him: and Abram was seventy and five years old when he departed out of Haran. (5) And Abram took Sarai his wife, and Lot his brother's son, and all their substance that they had gathered, and the souls that they had gotten in Haran: and they went forth to go into the land of Canaan; and into the land of Canaan they came. (6) And Abram passed through the land unto the

---
[1] Heb. *balal*, to confound.

place of Shechem, unto the [1] oak of Moreh. And the Canaanite was then in the land. (7) And the LORD appeared unto Abram, and said, Unto thy seed will I give this land: and there builded he an altar unto the LORD, who appeared unto him. (8) And he removed from thence unto the mountain on the east of Beth-el, and pitched his tent, having Beth-el on the west, and Ai on the east: and there he builded an altar unto the LORD, and called upon the name of the LORD. (9) And Abram journeyed, going on still toward the [2] South.

(10) And there was a famine in the land: and Abram went down into Egypt to sojourn there; for the famine was sore in the land. (11) And it came to pass, when he was come near to enter into Egypt, that he said unto Sarai his wife, Behold now, I know that thou art a fair woman to look upon: (12) and it shall come to pass, when the Egyptians shall see thee, that they shall say, This is his wife: and they will kill me, but they will save thee alive. (13) Say, I pray thee, thou art my sister: that it may be well with me for thy sake, and that my soul may live because of thee. (14) And it came to pass, that, when Abram was come into Egypt, the Egyptians beheld the woman that she was very fair. (15) And the princes of Pharaoh saw her, and praised her to Pharaoh: and the woman was taken into Pharaoh's house. (16) And he entreated Abram well for her sake: and he had sheep, and oxen, and he-asses, and menservants, and maidservants, and she-asses, and camels. (17) And the LORD plagued Pharaoh with great plagues because of Sarai Abram's wife. (18) And Pharaoh called Abram, and said, What is this that thou hast done unto me? why didst thou not tell me that she was thy wife? (19) Why saidst thou, She is my sister? so that I took her to be my wife: now therefore behold thy wife, take her, and go thy way. (20) And Pharaoh gave men charge concerning him: and they brought him on the way, and his wife, and all that he had.

13 And Abram went up out of Egypt, he, and his wife, and all that he had, into the South. (2) And Abram was very rich in cattle, in silver, and in gold. (3) And he went on his journeys from the South even to Beth-el, unto the place where his tent had been at the beginning, between Beth-el and Ai; (4) unto the place of the altar, which he had made there at the first: and there Abram called on the name of the LORD. (5) And Lot also, which went with Abram, had flocks, and herds, and tents. (6) And the land was not able to bear them, that they might dwell together: for their substance was great, so that they could not dwell together. (7) And there was a strife between the herdmen of Abram's cattle and the herdmen of Lot's cattle: and the Canaanite and the Perizzite dwelled then in the land. (8) And Abram said unto Lot, Let there be no strife, I pray thee, between me and thee, and between my herdmen and thy herdmen; for we are brethren. (9) Is not the whole land before thee? separate thyself, I pray thee, from me: if *thou wilt take* the left hand, then I will go to the right; or if *thou take* the right hand, then I will go to the left. (10) And Lot lifted up his eyes, and beheld all the [3] Plain of Jordan, that it was well watered every where, before the LORD destroyed Sodom and Gomorrah, like the garden of the LORD, like the land of Egypt, as thou goest unto Zoar. (11) So Lot chose him all the Plain of Jordan; and Lot journeyed east: and they separated themselves the one from the other. (12) Abram dwelled in the land of Canaan, and Lot dwelled in the cities of the Plain.

---

[1] *Or, terebinth.*   [2] Heb. *Negeb*, the southern tract of Judah.   [3] *Or, Circle.*

and moved his tent as far as Sodom. (13) Now the men of Sodom were wicked and sinners against the LORD exceedingly. (14) And the LORD said unto Abram, after that Lot was separated from him, Lift up now thine eyes, and look from the place where thou art, northward and southward and eastward and westward: (15) for all the land which thou seest, to thee will I give it, and to thy seed for ever. (16) And I will make thy seed as the dust of the earth: so that if a man can number the dust of the earth, then shall thy seed also be numbered. (17) Arise, walk through the land in the length of it and in the breadth of it; for unto thee will I give it. (18) And Abram moved his tent, and came and dwelt by the ¹ oaks of Mamre, which are in Hebron, and built there an altar unto the LORD.

14

---

¹ Or, *terebinths*. ² Or, *nations*. ³ Or, *joined themselves together against*. ⁴ Or, *the plain of Kiriathaim*.
⁵ Heb. *field*. ⁶ That is, *bitumen pits*. ⁷ Or, *north*. ⁸ Heb. *El Elyon*. ⁹ Or, *maker*.

GENESIS.

15 After these things the word of the Lord came unto Abram in a vision, saying, Fear not, Abram: I am thy shield, ⁴*and* thy exceeding great reward. (2) And Abram said, O Lord ⁵God, what wilt thou give me, seeing I ⁶go childless, and he that shall be possessor of my house is ⁷Dammesek Eliezer? (3) And Abram said, Behold, to me thou hast given no seed: and, lo, one born in my house is mine heir. (4) And, behold, the word of the Lord came unto him, saying, This man shall not be thine heir; but he that shall come forth out of thine own bowels shall be thine heir. (5) And he brought him forth abroad, and said, Look now toward heaven, and tell the stars, if thou be able to tell them: and he said unto him, So shall thy seed be. (6) And he believed in the Lord; and he counted it to him for righteousness. (7) And he said unto him, I am the Lord that brought thee out of Ur of the Chaldees, to give thee this land to inherit it. (8) And he said, Lord God, whereby shall I know that I shall inherit it? (9) And he said unto him, Take me an heifer of three years old, and a she-goat of three years old, and a ram of three years old, and a turtledove, and a young pigeon. (10) And he took him all these, and divided them in the midst, and laid each half over against the other: but the birds divided he not. (11) And the birds of prey came down upon the carcases, and Abram drove them away.

(17) And it came to pass, that, when the sun went down, and it was dark, behold a smoking furnace, and a flaming torch that passed between these pieces. (18) In that day the Lord made a covenant with Abram, saying, Unto thy seed have I given this land, from the river of Egypt unto the great river, the river Euphrates:

16 Now Sarai Abram's wife bare him no children: and she had an handmaid, an Egyptian, whose name was Hagar. (2) And Sarai said unto Abram, Behold now, the Lord hath restrained me from bearing; go in, I pray thee, unto my handmaid; it may be that I shall ⁸obtain children by her. And Abram hearkened to the voice of Sarai. (3) And Sarai Abram's wife took Hagar the Egyptian, her handmaid, after Abram had dwelt ten years in the land of Canaan, and gave her to Abram her husband to be his wife. (1)

---
¹ Heb. *El Elyon.* ² Or, *maker.* ³ Or, let there be *nothing for me: only that &c.* ⁴ Or, *thy reward shall be exceeding great.* ⁵ Heb. *Jehovah,* as in other places where God is put in capitals. ⁶ Or, *go hence.* ⁷ The Chaldee and Syriac have, *Eliezer the Damascene.* ⁸ Heb. *be builded by her.*

GENESIS. 15

And he went in unto Hagar, and she conceived: and when she saw that she had conceived, her mistress was despised in her eyes. (5) And Sarai said unto Abram, My wrong be upon thee: I gave my handmaid into thy bosom; and when she saw that she had conceived, I was despised in her eyes: the LORD judge between me and thee. (6) But Abram said unto Sarai, Behold, thy maid is in thy hand; do to her that which is good in thine eyes. And Sarai dealt hardly with her, and she fled from her face. (7) And the angel of the LORD found her by a fountain of water in the wilderness, by the fountain in the way to Shur. (8) And he said, Hagar, Sarai's handmaid, whence camest thou? and whither goest thou? And she said, I flee from the face of my mistress Sarai. (9) And the angel of the LORD said unto her, Return to thy mistress, and submit thyself under her hands. (10) And the angel of the LORD said unto her, I will greatly multiply thy seed, that it shall not be numbered for multitude. (11) And the angel of the LORD said unto her, Behold, thou art with child, and shalt bear a son; and thou shalt call his name ¹Ishmael, because the LORD hath heard thy affliction. (12) And he shall be *as* a wild-ass among men; his hand *shall be* against every man, and every man's hand against him; and he shall dwell ²in the presence of all his brethren. (13) And she called the name of the LORD that spake unto her, ³Thou art ⁴a God that seeth: for she said, Have I even here looked after him that seeth me? (14) Wherefore the well was called ⁵Beer-lahai-roi; behold, it is between Kadesh and Bered. (15) And Hagar bare Abram a son: and Abram called the name of his son, which Hagar bare, Ishmael. (16) And Abram was fourscore and six years old, when Hagar bare Ishmael to Abram.

17 And when Abram was ninety years old and nine, the LORD appeared to Abram, and said unto him, I am ⁶God Almighty; walk before me, and be thou perfect. (2) And I will make my covenant between me and thee, and will multiply thee exceedingly. (3) And Abram fell on his face: and God talked with him, saying, (4) As for me, behold, my covenant is with thee, and thou shalt be the father of a multitude of nations. (5) Neither shall thy name any more be called Abram, but thy name shall be Abraham; for the father of a multitude of nations have I made thee. (6) And I will make thee exceeding fruitful, and I will make nations of thee, and kings shall come out of thee. (7) And I will establish my covenant between me and thee and thy seed after thee throughout their generations for an everlasting covenant, to be a God unto thee and to thy seed after thee. (8) And I will give unto thee, and to thy seed after thee, the land of thy sojournings, all the land of Canaan, for an everlasting possession; and I will be their God. (9) And God said unto Abraham, And as for thee, thou shalt keep my covenant, thou, and thy seed after thee throughout their generations. (10) This is my covenant, which ye shall keep, between me and you and thy seed after thee; every male among you shall be circumcised. (11) And ye shall be circumcised in the flesh of your foreskin; and it shall be a token of a covenant betwixt me and you. (12) And he that is eight days old shall be circumcised among you, every male throughout your generations, he that is born in the house, or bought with money of any stranger, which is not of thy seed. (13) He that is born in thy house, and he that is bought with thy money, must needs be circumcised: and my covenant shall be in your flesh for an everlasting covenant. (14) And the uncircumcised male who is

---

¹ That is, *God heareth.* ² Or, *over against.* Or, *to the east of.* ³ Or, *Thou God seest me.* ⁴ Heb. *El roi, that is, God of seeing.* ⁵ That is, *The well of the living one who seeth me.* ⁶ Heb. *El Shaddai.*

not circumcised in the flesh of his foreskin, that soul shall be cut off from his people: he hath broken my covenant.

(15) And God said unto Abraham, As for Sarai thy wife, thou shalt not call her name Sarai, but [1] Sarah shall her name be. (16) And I will bless her, and moreover I will give thee a son of her: yea, I will bless her, and she shall be *a mother of nations*; kings of peoples shall be of her. (17) Then Abraham fell upon his face, and laughed, and said in his heart, Shall a child be born unto him that is an hundred years old? and shall Sarah, that is ninety years old, bear? (18) And Abraham, said unto God, Oh that Ishmael might live before thee! (19) And God said, Nay, but Sarah thy wife shall bear thee a son: and thou shalt call his name [2] Isaac: and I will establish my covenant with him for an everlasting covenant for his seed after him. (20) And as for Ishmael I have heard thee: behold, I have blessed him, and will make him fruitful, and will multiply him exceedingly; twelve princes shall he beget, and I will make him a great nation. (21) But my covenant will I establish with Isaac, which Sarah shall bear unto thee at this set time in the next year. (22) And he left off talking with him, and God went up from Abraham. (23) And Abraham took Ishmael his son, and all that were born in his house, and all that were bought with his money, every male among the men of Abraham's house, and circumcised the flesh of their foreskin in the selfsame day, as God had said unto him. (24) And Abraham was ninety years old and nine, when he was circumcised in the flesh of his foreskin. (25) And Ishmael his son was thirteen years old, when he was circumcised in the flesh of his foreskin. (26) In the selfsame day was Abraham circumcised, and Ishmael his son. (27) And all the men of his house, those born in the house, and those bought with money of the stranger, were circumcised with him.

18 And the LORD appeared unto him by the [3] oaks of Mamre, as he sat in the tent door in the heat of the day; (2) and he lift up his eyes and looked, and, lo, three men stood over against him: and when he saw them, he ran to meet them from the tent door, and bowed himself to the earth, (3) and said, ‘My lord, if now I have found favour in thy sight, pass not away, I pray thee, from thy servant: (4) let now a little water be fetched, and wash your feet, and rest yourselves under the tree: (5) and I will fetch a morsel of bread, and comfort ye your heart: after that ye shall pass on: [5] forasmuch as ye are come to your servant. And they said, So do, as thou hast said. (6) And Abraham hastened into the tent unto Sarah, and said, Make ready quickly three measures of fine meal, knead it, and make cakes. (7) And Abraham ran unto the herd, and fetched a calf tender and good, and gave it unto the servant: and he hasted to dress it. (8) And he took butter, and milk, and the calf which he had dressed, and set it before them; and he stood by them under the tree, and they did eat. (9) And they said unto him, Where is Sarah thy wife? And he said, Behold, in the tent. (10) And he said, I will certainly return unto thee when the season [6] cometh round; and, lo, Sarah thy wife shall have a son. And Sarah heard in the tent door, which was behind him. (11) Now Abraham and Sarah were old, *and* well stricken in age; it had ceased to be with Sarah after the manner of women. (12) And Sarah laughed within herself, saying, After I am waxed old shall I have pleasure, my lord being old also? (13) And the LORD said unto Abraham, Wherefore did Sarah laugh, saying, Shall I of a

---
[1] That is, *Princess*. [2] From the Heb. word meaning *to laugh*. [3] Or, *terebinths*. [4] Or, *O Lord*. [5] Or, *for therefore*. [6] Heb. *liveth*, or, *reviveth*.

surety bear a child, which am old? (14) Is any thing too ¹ hard for the LORD? At the set time I will return unto thee, when the season ² cometh round, and Sarah shall have a son. (15) Then Sarah denied, saying, I laughed not; for she was afraid. And he said, Nay; but thou didst laugh.

(16) And the men rose up from thence, and looked toward Sodom: and Abraham went with them to bring them on the way. (17) And the LORD said, Shall I hide from Abraham that thing which I do; (18) seeing that Abraham shall surely become a great and mighty nation, and all the nations of the earth shall be blessed in him? (19) For I know him, that he will command his children and his household after him, and they shall keep the way of the LORD, to do justice and judgment; that the LORD may bring upon Abraham that which he hath spoken of him. (20) And the LORD said, ⁴ Because the cry of Sodom and Gomorrah is great, and ⁴ because their sin is very grievous; (21) I will go down now, and see whether they have done altogether according to the cry of it, which is come unto me; and if not, I will know. (22) And the men turned from thence, and went toward Sodom: but Abraham stood yet before the LORD. (23) And Abraham drew near, and said, Wilt thou consume the righteous with the wicked? (24) Peradventure there be fifty righteous within the city: wilt thou consume and not spare the place for the fifty righteous that are therein? (25) That be far from thee to do after this manner, to slay the righteous with the wicked, that so the righteous should be as the wicked; that be far from thee: shall not the Judge of all the earth do right? (26) And the LORD said, If I find in Sodom fifty righteous within the city, then I will spare all the place for their sake. (27) And Abraham answered and said, Behold now, I have taken upon me to speak unto the Lord, which am but dust and ashes: (28) peradventure there shall lack five of the fifty righteous: wilt thou destroy all the city for lack of five? And he said, I will not destroy it, if I find there forty and five. (29) And he spake unto him yet again, and said, Peradventure there shall be forty found there. And he said, I will not do it for the forty's sake. (30) And he said, Oh let not the Lord be angry, and I will speak: peradventure there shall thirty be found there. And he said, I will not do it, if I find thirty there. (31) And he said, Behold now, I have taken upon me to speak unto the Lord: peradventure there shall be twenty found there. And he said, I will not destroy it for the twenty's sake. (32) And he said, Oh let not the Lord be angry, and I will speak yet but this once: peradventure ten shall be found there. And he said, I will not destroy it for the ten's sake. (33) And the LORD went his way, as soon as he had left communing with Abraham: and Abraham returned unto his place.

19 And the two angels came to Sodom at even; and Lot sat in the gate of Sodom: and Lot saw them, and rose up to meet them; and he bowed himself with his face to the earth; (2) and he said, Behold now, my lords, turn aside, I pray you, into your servant's house, and tarry all night, and wash your feet, and ye shall rise up early, and go on your way. And they said, Nay; but we will abide in the street all night. (3) And he urged them greatly; and they turned in unto him, and entered into his house; and he made them a feast, and did bake unleavened bread, and they did eat. (4) But before they lay down, the men of the city, *even the men of Sodom*, compassed the house round, both young and old, all the people from every quarter; (5) and they called unto Lot, and said unto him, Where are

---

¹ Or, *wonderful*.   ² Heb. *liveth*, or, *reviveth*.   ³ See Amos iii. 2.   ⁴ Or, *Verily*.

the men which came in to thee this night? bring them out unto us, that we may know them. (6) And Lot went out unto them to the door, and shut the door after him. (7) And he said, I pray you, my brethren, do not so wickedly. (8) Behold now, I have two daughters which have not known man; let me, I pray you, bring them out unto you, and do ye to them as is good in your eyes: only unto these men do nothing; ¹ forasmuch as they are come under the shadow of my roof. (9) And they said, Stand back. And they said, This one fellow came in to sojourn, and he will needs be a judge: now will we deal worse with thee, than with them. And they pressed sore upon the man, even Lot, and drew near to break the door. (10) But the men put forth their hand, and brought Lot into the house to them, and shut to the door. (11) And they smote the men that were at the door of the house with blindness, both small and great: so that they wearied themselves to find the door. (12) And the men said unto Lot, Hast thou here any besides? son in law, and thy sons, and thy daughters, and whomsoever thou hast in the city; bring them out of the place: (13) for we will destroy this place, because the cry of them is waxen great before the LORD; and the LORD hath sent us to destroy it. (14) And Lot went out, and spake unto his sons in law, which ² married his daughters, and said, Up, get you out of this place; for the LORD will destroy the city. But he seemed unto his sons in law as one that mocked. (15) And when the morning arose, then the angels hastened Lot, saying, Arise, take thy wife, and thy two daughters which are here; lest thou be consumed in the ³ iniquity of the city. (16) But he lingered; and the men laid hold upon his hand, and upon the hand of his wife, and upon the hand of his two daughters; the LORD being merciful unto him: and they brought him forth, and set him without the city. (17) And it came to pass, when they had brought them forth abroad, that he said, Escape for thy life; look not behind thee, neither stay thou in all the ⁴ Plain; escape to the mountain, lest thou be consumed. (18) And Lot said unto them, Oh, not so, ⁵ my lord: (19) behold now, thy servant hath found grace in thy sight, and thou hast magnified thy mercy, which thou hast shewed unto me in saving my life; and I cannot escape to the mountain, lest ⁶ evil overtake me, and I die: (20) behold now, this city is near to flee unto, and it is a little one: Oh, let me escape thither, (is it not a little one?) and my soul shall live. (21) And he said unto him, See, I have accepted thee concerning this thing also, that I will not overthrow the city of which thou hast spoken. (22) Haste thee, escape thither, for I cannot do any thing till thou be come thither. Therefore the name of the city was called ⁷ Zoar. (23) The sun was risen upon the earth when Lot came unto Zoar. (24) Then the LORD rained upon Sodom and upon Gomorrah brimstone and fire from the LORD out of heaven; (25) and he overthrew those cities, and all the Plain, and all the inhabitants of the cities, and that which grew upon the ground. (26) But his wife looked back from behind him, and she became a pillar of salt. (27) And Abraham gat up early in the morning to the place where he had stood before the LORD: (28) and he looked toward Sodom and Gomorrah, and toward all the land of the Plain, and beheld, and, lo, the smoke of the land went up as the smoke of a furnace.

(29) And it came to pass, when God destroyed the cities of the Plain, that God remembered Abraham, and sent Lot out of the midst of the overthrow, when

---

¹ Or, *for therefore.* ² Or, *were to marry.* ³ Or, *punishment.* ⁴ See ch. xiii. 10. ⁵ Or, *O Lord.* ⁶ Or, *the evil.* ⁷ That is, *Little*, ver. 20. See ch. xiv. 8.

GENESIS.

overthrew the cities in the which Lot dwelt.

(30) And Lot went up out of Zoar, and dwelt in the mountain, and his two daughters with him; for he feared to dwell in Zoar: and he dwelt in a cave, he and his two daughters. (31) And the firstborn said unto the younger, Our father is old, and there is not a man in the earth to come in unto us after the manner of all the earth: (32) come, let us make our father drink wine, and we will lie with him, that we may preserve seed of our father.

And they made their father drink wine that night: and the firstborn went in, and lay with her father; and he knew not when she lay down, nor when she arose.

And it came to pass on the morrow, that the firstborn said unto the younger, Behold, I lay yesternight with my father: let us make him drink wine this night also; and go thou in, and lie with him, that we may preserve seed of our father. (35) And they made their father drink wine that night also: and the younger arose, and lay with him; and he knew not when she lay down, nor when she arose. (36) Thus were both the daughters of Lot with child by their father. (37) And the firstborn bare a son, and called his name Moab: the same is the father of the Moabites unto this day. (38) And the younger, she also bare a son, and called his name Ben-ammi: the same is the father of the children of Ammon unto this day.

20 And A b r a h a m journeyed from thence toward the land of the South, and dwelt between Kadesh and Shur; and he sojourned in Gerar. (2) And Abraham said of Sarah his wife, She is my sister: and Abimelech king of Gerar sent, and took Sarah. (3) But God came to Abimelech in a dream of the night, and said to him, Behold, thou art but a dead man, because of the woman which thou hast taken; for she is a man's wife. (4) Now Abimelech had not come near her: and he said, Lord, wilt thou slay even a righteous nation? (5) Said he not himself unto me, She is my sister? and she, even she herself said, He is my brother: in the integrity of my heart and the innocency of my hands have I done this. (6) And God said unto him in the dream, Yea, I know that in the integrity of thy heart thou hast done this, and I also withheld thee from sinning against me: therefore suffered I thee not to touch her. (7) Now therefore restore the man's wife; for he is a prophet, and he shall pray for thee, and thou shalt live: and if thou restore her not, know thou that thou shalt surely die, thou, and all that are thine. (8) And Abimelech rose early in the morning, and called all his servants, and told all these things in their ears: and the men were sore afraid. (9) Then Abimelech called Abraham, and said unto him, What hast thou done unto us? and wherein have I sinned against thee, that thou hast brought on me and on my kingdom a great sin? thou hast done deeds unto me that ought not to be done. (10) And Abimelech said unto Abraham, What sawest thou, that thou hast done this thing? (11) And Abraham said, Because I thought, Surely the fear of God is not in this place; and they will slay me for my wife's sake. (12) And moreover she is indeed my sister, the daughter of my father, but not the daughter of my mother; and she became my wife: (13) and it came to pass, when God caused me to wander from my father's house, that I said unto her, This is thy kindness which thou shalt shew unto me; at every place whither we shall come, say of me, He is my brother. (14) And Abimelech took sheep and oxen, and menservants and womenservants, and gave them unto Abraham, and restored him Sarah his wife. (15) And Abimelech said, Behold, my land is before thee: dwell where it pleaseth thee. (16) And unto Sarah he said, Behold, I have given thy brother a thousand pieces of silver; behold, ¹ it is for thee a covering of the eyes to all that are with thee; and ² in respect of all thou art righted. (17) And Abraham prayed unto God: and God healed Abimelech, and his wife, and his maidservants; and they bare children. (1 For the Lord had fast the wombs of the house of ... cause of Sarah Abraham's ...)

(21) **And the LORD visited Sarah as he had said,** and the Lord did unto Sarah as he had spoken. (2) And Sarah conceived, and bare Abraham a son in his old age, at the set time of which God had spoken to him. (3) And Abraham called the name of his son that was born unto him, whom Sarah bare to him, Isaac. (4) And Abraham circumcised his son Isaac when he was eight days old, as God had commanded him. (5) And Abraham was an hundred years old, when his son Isaac was born unto him. (6) And Sarah said, God hath ³ made me to laugh; every one that heareth will laugh with me. (7) And she said, Who would have said unto Abraham, that Sarah should give children suck? for I have borne him a son in his old age.

(8) And the child grew, and was weaned: and Abraham made a great feast on the day that Isaac was weaned. (9) And Sarah saw the son of Hagar the Egyptian, which she had borne unto Abraham, ⁴ mocking. (10) Wherefore she said unto Abraham, Cast out this bondwoman and her son: for the son of this bondwoman shall not be heir with my son, even with Isaac. (11) And the thing was very grievous in Abraham's sight on account of his son. (12) And God said unto Abraham, Let it not be grievous in thy sight because of the lad, and because of thy bondwoman; in all that Sarah saith unto thee, hearken unto her voice; for in Isaac shall thy seed be called. (13) And also of the son of the bondwoman will I make a nation, because he is thy seed. (14) And Abraham rose up early in the morning, and took bread and a ⁵ bottle of water, and gave it unto Hagar, putting it on her shoulder, and the child, and sent her away: and she departed, and wandered in the wilderness of Beer-sheba. (15) And the water in the bottle was spent, and she cast the child under one of the shrubs. (16) And she went, and sat her down over against him a good way off, as it were a bowshot: for she said, Let me not look upon the death of the child. And she sat over against him, and lift up her voice, and wept. (17) And God heard the voice of the lad; and the angel of God called to Hagar out of heaven, and said unto her, What aileth thee, Hagar? fear not: for God hath heard the voice of the lad where he is. (18) Arise, lift up the lad, and hold him in thine hand; for I will make him a great nation. (19) And God opened her eyes, and she saw a well of water; and she went, and filled the bottle with water, and gave the lad drink. (20) And God was with the lad, and he grew; and he dwelt in the wilderness, and ⁶ became an archer. (21) And he dwelt in the wilderness of Paran: and his mother took him a wife out of the land of Egypt.

(22) And it came to pass at that time, that Abimelech and Phicol the captain of his host spake unto Abraham, saying, God is with thee in all that thou doest: (23) now therefore swear unto me here by God that thou wilt not deal falsely with me, nor with ⁷ my son, nor with my son's son: but according to the kindness that I have done unto thee, thou shalt do unto me, and to the land wherein thou hast sojourned. (24) And Abraham said, I will swear. (25) And Abraham reproved Abimelech because of the well of water, which Abimelech's servants had violently

---

¹ Or, he. ² Or, before all men. ³ Or, prepared laughter for me. ⁴ Or, playing. ⁵ Or, skin. ⁶ Or, became, as he grew up, an archer. ⁷ Or, my offspring, nor with my posterity.

taken away. (26) And Abimelech said, I know not who hath done this thing: neither didst thou tell me, neither yet heard I of it, but to-day. (27) And Abraham took sheep and oxen, and gave them unto Abimelech; and they two made a covenant. (28) And Abraham set seven ewe lambs of the flock by themselves. (29) And Abimelech said unto Abraham, What mean these seven ewe lambs which thou hast set by themselves? (30) And he said, These seven ewe lambs shalt thou take of my hand, that it may be a witness unto me, that I have digged this well. (31) Wherefore he called that place Beer-sheba; because there they sware both of them. (32) So they made a covenant at Beer-sheba: and Abimelech rose up, and Phicol the captain of his host, and they returned into the land of the Philistines. (33) And *Abraham* planted a tamarisk tree in Beer-sheba, and called there on the name of the LORD, the Everlasting God. (34) And Abraham sojourned in the land of the Philistines many days.

22 And it came to pass after these things, that God did prove Abraham, and said unto him, Abraham; and he said, Here am I. (2) And he said, Take now thy son, thine only son, whom thou lovest, even Isaac, and get thee into the land of Moriah; and offer him there for a burnt offering upon one of the mountains which I will tell thee of. (3) And Abraham rose early in the morning, and saddled his ass, and took two of his young men with him, and Isaac his son; and he clave the wood for the burnt offering, and rose up, and went unto the place of which God had told him. (4) On the third day Abraham lifted up his eyes, and saw the place afar off. (5) And Abraham said unto his young men, Abide ye here with the ass, and I and the lad will go yonder; and we will worship, and come again to you. (6) And Abraham took the wood of the burnt offering, and laid it upon Isaac his son; and he took in his hand the fire and the knife; and they went both of them together. (7) And Isaac spake unto Abraham his father, and said, My father: and he said, Here am I, my son. And he said, Behold, the fire and the wood: but where is the lamb for a burnt offering? (8) And Abraham said, God will [1] provide himself the lamb for a burnt offering, my son: so they went both of them together. (9) And they came to the place which God had told him of; and Abraham built the altar there, and laid the wood in order, and bound Isaac his son, and laid him on the altar, upon the wood. (10) And Abraham stretched forth his hand, and took the knife to slay his son. (11) And the angel of the LORD called unto him out of heaven, and said, Abraham, Abraham: and he said, Here am I. (12) And he said, Lay not thine hand upon the lad, neither do thou any thing unto him: for now I know that thou fearest God, seeing thou hast not withheld thy son, thine only son, from me. (13) And Abraham lifted up his eyes, and looked, and [2] behold, behind *him* a ram caught in the thicket by his horns: and Abraham went and took the ram, and offered him up for a burnt offering in the stead of his son. (14) And Abraham called the name of that place [3] Jehovah-jireh: as it is said to this day, In the mount of the LORD [4] it shall be provided. (15) And the angel of the LORD called unto Abraham a second time out of heaven, (16) and said, By myself have I sworn, saith the LORD, because thou hast done this thing, and hast not withheld thy son, thine only son: (17) that in blessing I will bless thee, and in multiplying I will multiply thy seed as the stars of the heaven, and as the sand which is upon

---

[1] Heb. *see for himself.* [2] Or, according to many ancient authorities, *behold a* (Heb. *one*) *ram caught.* [3] That is, The LORD *will see,* or, *provide.* [4] Or, *he shall be seen.*

[...] shore; and thy seed shall possess [...] gate of his enemies; (18) and in thy [...] all the nations of the earth be [...] because thou hast obeyed my voice. (19) So Abraham returned unto his young men, and they rose up and went together to Beer-sheba; and Abraham dwelt at Beer-sheba.

(20) And it came to pass after these things, that it was told Abraham, saying, Behold, Milcah, she also hath borne children unto thy brother Nahor; (21) Uz his firstborn, and Buz his brother, and Kemuel the father of Aram; (22) and Chesed, and Hazo, and Pildash, and Jidlaph, and Bethuel. (23) And Bethuel begat Rebekah: these eight did Milcah bear to Nahor, Abraham's brother. (24) And his concubine, whose name was Reumah, she also bare Tebah, and Gaham, and Tahash, and Maacah.

23 And the life of Sarah was an hundred and seven and twenty years: these were the years of the life of Sarah. (2) And Sarah died in Kiriath-arba (the same is Hebron), in the land of Canaan: and Abraham came to mourn for Sarah, and to weep for her. (3) And Abraham rose up from before his dead, and spake unto the children of Heth, saying, (4) I am a stranger and a sojourner with you: give me a possession of a buryingplace with you, that I may bury my dead out of my sight. (5) And the children of Heth answered Abraham, saying unto him, (6) Hear us, my lord: thou art [2] a mighty prince among us: in the choice of our sepulchres bury thy dead; none of us shall withhold from thee his sepulchre, but that thou mayest bury thy dead. (7) And Abraham rose up, and bowed himself to the people of the land, even to the children of Heth. (8) And he communed with them, saying, If it be your mind that I should bury my dead out of my sight, hear me, and intreat for me to Ephron the son of Zohar, (9) that he may give me the cave of Machpelah, which he hath, which is in the end of his field; for the full price let him give it to me in the midst of you for a possession of a buryingplace. (10) Now Ephron was sitting in the midst of the children of Heth: and Ephron the Hittite answered Abraham in the audience of the children of Heth, even of all that went in at the gate of his city, saying, (11) Nay, my lord, hear me: the field give I thee, and the cave that is therein, I give it thee; in the presence of the sons of my people give I it thee: bury thy dead. (12) And Abraham bowed himself down before the people of the land. (13) And he spake unto Ephron in the audience of the people of the land, saying, But if thou wilt, I pray thee, hear me: I will give the price of the field; take it of me, and I will bury my dead there. (14) And Ephron answered Abraham, saying unto him, (15) My lord, hearken unto me: a piece of land worth four hundred shekels of silver, what is that betwixt me and thee? bury therefore thy dead. (16) And Abraham hearkened unto Ephron; and Abraham weighed to Ephron the silver, which he had named in the audience of the children of Heth, four hundred shekels of silver, current *money* with the merchant. (17) So the field of Ephron, which was in Machpelah, which was before Mamre, the field, and the cave which was therein, and all the trees that were in the field, that were in all the border thereof round about, were made sure (18) unto Abraham for a possession in the presence of the children of Heth, before all that went in at the gate of his city. (19) And after this, Abraham buried Sarah his wife in the cave of the field of Machpelah before Mamre (the same is Hebron), in the land of Canaan. (20) And the field, and the cave that is therein, were made sure unto Abraham for a

---

[1] *Or, bless themselves.*   [2] Heb. *a prince of God.*

possession of a buryingplace by the children of Heth.

24 And Abraham was old, *and* well stricken in age: and the LORD had blessed Abraham in all things. (2) And Abraham said unto his servant, the elder of his house, that ruled over all that he had, Put, I pray thee, thy hand under my thigh: (3) and I will make thee swear by the LORD, the God of heaven and the God of the earth, that thou shalt not take a wife for my son of the daughters of the Canaanites, among whom I dwell: (4) but thou shalt go unto my country, and to my kindred, and take a wife for my son Isaac. (5) And the servant said unto him, Peradventure the woman will not be willing to follow me unto this land: must I needs bring thy son again unto the land from whence thou camest? (6) And Abraham said unto him, Beware thou that thou bring not my son thither again. (7) The LORD, the God of heaven, that took me from my father's house, and from the land of my nativity, and that spake unto me, and that sware unto me, saying, Unto thy seed will I give this land; he shall send his angel before thee, and thou shalt take a wife for my son from thence. (8) And if the woman be not willing to follow thee, then thou shalt be clear from this my oath; only thou shalt not bring my son thither again. (9) And the servant put his hand under the thigh of Abraham his master, and sware to him concerning this matter. (10) And the servant took ten camels, of the camels of his master, and departed; ¹having all goodly things of his master's in his hand: and he arose, and went to ²Mesopotamia, unto the city of Nahor. (11) And he made the camels to kneel down without the city by the well of water at the time of evening, the time that women go out to draw water. (12) And he said, O LORD, the God of my master Abraham, send me, I pray thee, good speed this day, and shew kindness unto my master Abraham. (13) Behold, I stand by the fountain of water; and the daughters of the men of the city come out to draw water: (14) and let it come to pass, that the damsel to whom I shall say, Let down thy pitcher, I pray thee, that I may drink; and she shall say, Drink, and I will give thy camels drink also: let the same be she that thou hast appointed for thy servant Isaac; and thereby shall I know that thou hast shewed kindness unto my master. (15) And it came to pass, before he had done speaking, that, behold, Rebekah came out, who was born to Bethuel the son of Milcah, the wife of Nahor, Abraham's brother, with her pitcher upon her shoulder. (16) And the damsel was very fair to look upon, a virgin, neither had any man known her: and she went down to the fountain, and filled her pitcher, and came up. (17) And the servant ran to meet her, and said, Give me to drink, I pray thee, a little water of thy pitcher. (18) And she said, Drink, my lord: and she hasted, and let down her pitcher upon her hand, and gave him drink. (19) And when she had done giving him drink, she said, I will draw for thy camels also, until they have done drinking. (20) And she hasted, and emptied her pitcher into the trough, and ran again unto the well to draw, and drew for all his camels. (21) And the man looked stedfastly on her; holding his peace, to know whether the LORD had made his journey prosperous or not. (22) And it came to pass, as the camels had done drinking, that the man took a golden ring of ³half a shekel weight, and two bracelets for her hands of ten shekels weight of gold; (23) and said, Whose daughter art thou? tell me, I pray thee. Is there room in thy father's house for us to lodge in? (24) And she said

---

¹ Or, *for all the goods of his master were in his hand.*
² Heb. *a beka.* See Ex. xxxviii. 26.
³ Heb. *Aram-naharaim, that is, Aram of the two rivers.*

unto him, I am the daughter of Bethuel the son of Milcah, which she bare unto Nahor. (25) She said moreover unto him, We have both straw and provender enough, and room to lodge in. (26) And the man bowed his head, and worshipped the LORD. (27) And he said, Blessed be the LORD, the God of my master Abraham, who hath not forsaken his mercy and his truth toward my master: as for me, the LORD hath led me in the way to the house of my master's brethren. (28) And the damsel ran, and told her mother's house according to these words. (29) And Rebekah had a brother, and his name was Laban: and Laban ran out unto the man, unto the fountain. (30) And it came to pass, when he saw the ring, and the bracelets upon his sister's hands, and when he heard the words of Rebekah his sister, saying, Thus spake the man unto me; that he came unto the man; and, behold, he stood by the camels at the fountain. (31) And he said, Come in, thou blessed of the LORD; wherefore standest thou without? for I have prepared the house, and room for the camels. (32) And the man came into the house, and he ungirded the camels; and he gave straw and provender for the camels, and water to wash his feet and the men's feet that were with him. (33) And there was set meat before him to eat: but he said, I will not eat, until I have told mine errand. And he said, Speak on. (34) And he said, I am Abraham's servant. (35) And the LORD hath blessed my master greatly; and he is become great: and he hath given him flocks and herds, and silver and gold, and menservants and maidservants, and camels and asses. (36) And Sarah my master's wife bare a son to my master when she was old: and unto him hath he given all that he hath. (37) And my master made me swear, saying, Thou shalt not take a wife for my son of the daughters of the Canaanites, in whose land I dwell: (38) but thou shalt go unto my father's house, and to my kindred, and take a wife for my son. (39) And I said unto my master, Peradventure the woman will not follow me. (40) And he said unto me, The LORD, before whom I walk, will send his angel with thee, and prosper thy way; and thou shalt take a wife for my son of my kindred, and of my father's house: (41) then shalt thou be clear from my oath, when thou comest to my kindred; and if they give her not to thee, thou shalt be clear from my oath. (42) And I came this day unto the fountain, and said, O LORD, the God of my master Abraham, if now thou do prosper my way which I go: (43) behold, I stand by the fountain of water; and let it come to pass, that the maiden which cometh forth to draw, to whom I shall say, Give me, I pray thee, a little water of thy pitcher to drink; (44) and she shall say to me, Both drink thou, and I will also draw for thy camels: let the same be the woman whom the LORD hath appointed for my master's son. (45) And before I had done speaking in mine heart, behold, Rebekah came forth with her pitcher on her shoulder; and she went down unto the fountain, and drew: and I said unto her, Let me drink, I pray thee. (46) And she made haste, and let down her pitcher from her shoulder, and said, Drink, and I will give thy camels drink also: so I drank, and she made the camels drink also. (47) And I asked her, and said, Whose daughter art thou? And she said, The daughter of Bethuel, Nahor's son, whom Milcah bare unto him: and I put the ring upon her nose, and the bracelets upon her hands. (48) And I bowed my head, and worshipped the LORD, and blessed the LORD, the God of my master Abraham, which had led me in the right way to take my master's brother's daughter for his son. (49) And now if ye will deal kindly and truly with my master, tell me: and if not, tell me; that I may turn to the right hand, or to the left. (50)

Then Laban and Bethuel answered and said, The thing proceedeth from the LORD: we cannot speak unto thee bad or good. (51) Behold, Rebekah is before thee, take her, and go, and let her be thy master's son's wife, as the LORD hath spoken. (52) And it came to pass, that, when Abraham's servant heard their words, he bowed himself down to the earth unto the LORD. (53) And the servant brought forth jewels of silver, and jewels of gold, and raiment, and gave them to Rebekah: he gave also to her brother and to her mother precious things. (54) And they did eat and drink, he and the men that were with him, and tarried all night; and they rose up in the morning, and he said, Send me away unto my master. (55) And her brother and her mother said, Let the damsel abide with us *a few* days, at the least ten ; after that she shall go. (56) And he said unto them, Hinder me not, seeing the LORD hath prospered my way; send me away that I may go to my master. (57) And they said, We will call the damsel, and inquire at her mouth. (58) And they called Rebekah, and said unto her, Wilt thou go with this man? And she said, I will go. (59) And they sent away Rebekah their sister, and her nurse, and Abraham's servant, and his men. (60) And they blessed Rebekah, and said unto her, Our sister, be thou *the mother* of thousands of ten thousands, and let thy seed possess the gate of those which hate them. (61) And Rebekah arose, and her damsels, and they rode upon the camels, and followed the man: and the servant took Rebekah, and went his way. (62) And Isaac came [1] from the way of Beer-lahai-roi; for he dwelt in the land of the South. (63) And Isaac went out to meditate in the field at the eventide: and he lifted up his eyes, and saw, and, behold, there were camels coming. (64) And Rebekah lifted up her eyes, and when she saw Isaac, she lighted off the camel. (65) And she said unto the servant, What man is this that walketh in the field to meet us? And the servant said, It is my master: and she took her veil, and covered herself. (66) And the servant told Isaac all the things that he had done. (67) And Isaac brought her into his mother Sarah's tent, and took Rebekah, and she became his wife; and he loved her: and Isaac was comforted after his mother's death.

25 And Abraham took another wife, and her name was Keturah. (2) And she bare him Zimran, and Jokshan, and Medan, and Midian, and Ishbak, and Shuah. (3) And Jokshan begat Sheba, and Dedan. And the sons of Dedan were Asshurim, and Letushim, and Leummim. (4) And the sons of Midian; Ephah, and Epher, and Hanoch, and Abida, and Eldaah. All these were the children of Keturah. (5) And Abraham gave all that he had unto Isaac. (6) But unto the sons of the concubines, which Abraham had, Abraham gave gifts: and he sent them away from Isaac his son, while he yet lived, eastward, unto the east country. (7) And these are the days of the years of Abraham's life which he lived, an hundred threescore and fifteen years. (8) And Abraham gave up the ghost, and died in a good old age, an old man, and full *of years;* and was gathered to his people. (9) And Isaac and Ishmael his sons buried him in the cave of Machpelah, in the field of Ephron the son of Zohar the Hittite, which is before Mamre ; (10) the field which Abraham purchased of the children of Heth: there was Abraham buried, and Sarah his wife. (11) And it came to pass after the death of Abraham, that God blessed Isaac his son; and Isaac dwelt by Beer-lahai-roi.

(12) Now these are the generations of Ishmael, Abraham's son, whom Hagar the Egyptian, Sarah's handmaid, bare un-

---
[1] The Sept. has, *through the wilderness.*

to Abraham: (13) and these are the names of the sons of Ishmael, by their names, according to their generations: the firstborn of Ishmael, Nebaioth; and Kedar, and Adbeel, (14) and Mibsam, and Mishma, and Dumah, and Massa; (15) Hadad, and Tema, Jetur, Naphish, and Kedemah: (16) these are the sons of Ishmael, and these are their names, by their villages, and by their encampments; twelve princes according to their nations. (17) And these are the years of the life of Ishmael, an hundred and thirty and seven years: and he gave up the ghost and died: and was gathered unto his people. (18) And they dwelt from Havilah unto Shur that is before Egypt, as thou goest toward Assyria: he ¹ abode ²in the presence of all his brethren.

(19) And these are the generations of Isaac, Abraham's son: Abraham begat Isaac: (20) and Isaac was forty years old when he took Rebekah, the daughter of Bethuel the ³Syrian of Paddan-aram, the sister of Laban the ³Syrian, to be his wife. (21) And Isaac intreated the LORD for his wife, because she was barren: and the LORD was intreated of him, and Rebekah his wife conceived. (22) And the children struggled together within her; and she said, If it be so, ⁴ wherefore do I live? And she went to inquire of the LORD. (23) And the LORD said unto her,

Two nations are in thy womb,
And two peoples shall be separated even from thy bowels:
And the one people shall be stronger than the other people;
And the elder shall serve the younger.

(24) And when her days to be delivered were fulfilled, behold, there were twins in her womb. (25) And the first came forth ⁵ red, all over like an hairy garment; and they called his name Esau. (26) And after that came forth his brother, and his hand had hold on Esau's heel; and his name was called ⁶Jacob: and Isaac was threescore years old when she bare them. (27) And the boys grew: and Esau was a cunning hunter, a man of the field; and Jacob was a ⁷ plain man, dwelling in tents. (28) Now Isaac loved Esau, because he did eat of his venison: and Rebekah loved Jacob. (29) And Jacob sod pottage: and Esau came in from the field, and he was faint: (30) and Esau said to Jacob, Feed me, I pray thee, with ⁸ that same red pottage; for I am faint: therefore was his name called ⁹Edom. (31) And Jacob said, Sell me ¹⁰ this day thy birthright. (32) And Esau said, Behold, I am at the point to die: and what profit shall the birthright do to me? (33) And Jacob said, Swear to me ¹⁰ this day; and he sware unto him: and he sold his birthright unto Jacob. (34) And Jacob gave Esau bread and pottage of lentils; and he did eat and drink, and rose up, and went his way: so Esau despised his birthright.

26 And there was a famine in the land, beside the first famine that was in the days of Abraham. And Isaac went unto Abimelech king of the Philistines unto Gerar. (2) And the LORD appeared unto him, and said, Go not down into Egypt; dwell in the land which I shall tell thee of: (3) sojourn in this land, and I will be with thee, and will bless thee: for unto thee and unto thy seed, I will give all these lands and I will establish the oath which I sware unto Abraham thy father. (4) and I will multiply thy seed as the stars of heaven and will give unto thy seed all these lands and in thy seed shall all the nations of the earth ¹¹ be blessed: (5) because that Abraham obeyed my voice, and kept my charge, my commandments, my statutes, and my laws. (6) And Isaac dwelt in Gerar: (7) and the men of the place asked him of his wife; and he said, She

¹ Or, settled. Heb. fell. ² Or, over against. ³ Heb. Aramean. ⁴ Or, wherefore am I thus? ⁵ Or, ruddy. ⁶ That is, One that takes by the heel or supplants. ⁷ Or, quiet. Or, harmless. Heb. perfect. ⁸ Heb. the red pottage, this red pottage. ⁹ That is, Red. ¹⁰ Or, first of all. ¹¹ Or, bless themselves.

is my sister: for he feared to say, My wife; lest, *said he*, the men of the place should kill me for Rebekah: because she was fair to look upon. (8) And it came to pass, when he had been there a long time, that Abimelech king of the Philistines looked out at a window, and saw, and, behold, Isaac was sporting with Rebekah his wife. (9) And Abimelech called Isaac, and said, Behold, of a surety she is thy wife: and how saidst thou, She is my sister? And Isaac said unto him, Because I said, Lest I die for her. (10) And Abimelech said, What is this thou hast done unto us? one of the people might lightly have lien with thy wife, and thou shouldest have brought guiltiness upon us. (11) And Abimelech charged all the people, saying, He that toucheth this man or his wife shall surely be put to death. (12) And Isaac sowed in that land, and found in the same year an hundredfold: and the LORD blessed him. (13) And the man waxed great, and grew more and more until he became very great: (14) and he had possessions of flocks, and possessions of herds, and a great household: and the Philistines envied him. (15) Now all the wells which his father's servants had digged in the days of Abraham his father, the Philistines had stopped them, and filled them with earth. (16) And Abimelech said unto Isaac, Go from us; for thou art much mightier than we. (17) And Isaac departed thence, and encamped in the valley of Gerar, and dwelt there. (18) And Isaac digged again the wells of water, which they had digged in the days of Abraham his father; for the Philistines had stopped them after the death of Abraham: and he called their names after the names by which his father had called them. (19) And Isaac's servants digged in the valley, and found there a well of ¹ springing water. (20) And the herdmen of Gerar strove with Isaac's herdmen, saying, The water is ours: and he called the name of the well ² Esek; because they contended with him. (21) And they digged another well, and they strove for that also: and he called the name of it ³ Sitnah. (22) And he removed from thence, and digged another well; and for that they strove not: and he called the name of it ⁴ Rehoboth; and he said, For now the LORD hath made room for us, and we shall be fruitful in the land. (23) And he went up from thence to Beer-sheba. (24) And the LORD appeared unto him the same night, and said, I am the God of Abraham thy father: fear not, for I am with thee, and will bless thee, and multiply thy seed for my servant Abraham's sake. (25) And he builded an altar there, and called upon the name of the LORD, and pitched his tent there: and there Isaac's servants digged a well. (26) Then Abimelech went to him from Gerar, and Ahuzzath his friend, and Phicol the captain of his host. (27) And Isaac said unto them, Wherefore are ye come unto me, seeing ye hate me, and have sent me away from you? (28) And they said, We saw plainly that the LORD was with thee: and we said, Let there now be an oath betwixt us, even betwixt us and thee, and let us make a covenant with thee; (29) that thou wilt do us no hurt, as we have not touched thee, and as we have done unto thee nothing but good, and have sent thee away in peace: thou art now the blessed of the LORD. (30) And he made them a feast, and they did eat and drink. (31) And they rose up betimes in the morning, and sware one to another: and Isaac sent them away, and they departed from him in peace. (32) And it came to pass the same day, that Isaac's servants came, and told him concerning the well which they had digged, and said unto him, We have found water. (33) And he called it ⁵ Shibah: therefore

---

¹ Heb. *living*. ² That is, *Contention*. ³ That is, *Enmity*. ⁴ That is, *Broad places*, or, *Room*. ⁵ See ch. xxi. 31.

the name of the city is Beer-sheba unto this day. (34) And when Esau was forty years old he took to wife Judith the daughter of Beeri the Hittite, and Basemath the daughter of Elon the Hittite: (35) and they were ¹a grief of mind unto Isaac and to Rebekah.

27 And it came to pass, that when Isaac was old, and his eyes were dim, so that he could not see, he called Esau his elder son, and said unto him, My son: and he said unto him, Here am I. (2) And he said, Behold now, I am old, I know not the day of my death. (3) Now therefore take, I pray thee, thy weapons, thy quiver and thy bow, and go out to the field, and take me venison; (4) and make me savoury meat, such as I love, and bring it to me, that I may eat; that my soul may bless thee before I die. (5) And Rebekah heard when Isaac spake to Esau his son. And Esau went to the field to hunt for venison, and to bring it. (6) And Rebekah spake unto Jacob her son, saying, Behold, I heard thy father speak unto Esau thy brother, saying, (7) Bring me venison, and make me savoury meat, that I may eat, and bless thee before the LORD before my death. (8) Now therefore, my son, obey my voice according to that which I command thee. (9) Go now to the flock, and fetch me from thence two good kids of the goats; and I will make them savoury meat for thy father, such as he loveth: (10) and thou shalt bring it to thy father, that he may eat, so that he may bless thee before his death. (11) And Jacob said to Rebekah his mother, Behold, Esau my brother is a hairy man, and I am a smooth man. (12) My father peradventure will feel me, and I shall seem to him as a ²deceiver: and I shall bring a curse upon me, and not a blessing. (13) And his mother said unto him, Upon me be thy curse, my son: only obey my voice, and go fetch me them. (14) And he went, and fetched, and brought them to his mother: and his mother made savoury meat, such as his father loved. (15) And Rebekah took the goodly raiment of Esau her elder son, which were with her in the house, and put them upon Jacob her younger son: (16) and she put the skins of the kids of the goats upon his hands, and upon the smooth of his neck: (17) and she gave the savoury meat and the bread, which she had prepared, into the hand of her son Jacob. (18) And he came unto his father, and said, My father: and he said, Here am I; who art thou, my son? (19) And Jacob said unto his father, I am Esau thy firstborn; I have done according as thou badest me: arise, I pray thee, sit and eat of my venison, that thy soul may bless me. (20) And Isaac said unto his son, How is it that thou hast found it so quickly, my son? And he said, Because the LORD thy God sent me good speed. (21) And Isaac said unto Jacob, Come near, I pray thee, that I may feel thee, my son, whether thou be my very son Esau or not. (22) And Jacob went near unto Isaac his father; and he felt him, and said, The voice is Jacob's voice, but the hands are the hands of Esau. (23) And he discerned him not, because his hands were hairy, as his brother Esau's hands: so he blessed him. (24) And he said, Art thou my very son Esau? And he said, I am. (25) And he said, Bring it near to me, and I will eat of my son's venison, that my soul may bless thee. And he brought it near to him, and he did eat: and he brought him wine, and he drank. (26) And his father Isaac said unto him, Come near now, and kiss me, my son. (27) And he came near, and kissed him: and he smelled the smell of his raiment, and blessed him, and said,

See, the smell of my son

---

¹ Heb. *bitterness of spirit*. ² Or, *mocker*.

Is as the smell of a field which the Lord hath blessed: (28) And God give thee of the dew of heaven,

And of the fatness of the earth,
And plenty of corn and wine:
(29) Let peoples serve thee,
And nations bow down to thee:
Be lord over thy brethren,
And let thy mother's sons bow down to thee:
Cursed be every one that curseth thee,
And blessed be every one that blesseth thee.

(30) And it came to pass, as soon as Isaac had made an end of blessing Jacob, and Jacob was yet scarce gone out from the presence of Isaac his father, that Esau his brother came in from his hunting. (31) And he also made savoury meat, and brought it unto his father; and he said unto his father, Let my father arise, and eat of his son's venison, that thy soul may bless me. (32) And Isaac his father said unto him, Who art thou? And he said, I am thy son, thy firstborn, Esau. (33) And Isaac trembled very exceedingly, and said, Who then is he that hath taken venison, and brought it me, and I have eaten of all before thou camest, and have blessed him? yea, and he shall be blessed. (34) When Esau heard the words of his father, he cried with an exceeding great and bitter cry, and said unto his father, Bless me, even me also, O my father. (35) And he said, Thy brother came with guile, and hath taken away thy blessing. (36) And he said, Is not he rightly named ¹Jacob? for he hath supplanted me these two times: he took away my birthright; and, behold, now he hath taken away my blessing. And he said, Hast thou not reserved a blessing for me? (37) And Isaac answered and said unto Esau, Behold, I have made him thy lord, and all his brethren have I given to him for servants; and with corn and wine have I sustained him: and what then shall I do for thee, my son? (38) And Esau said unto his father, Hast thou but one blessing, my father? bless me, even me also, O my father. And Esau lifted up his voice, and wept. (39) And Isaac his father answered and said unto him,

Behold, ²of the fatness of the earth shall be thy dwelling,
And ²of the dew of heaven from above:
(40) And by thy sword shalt thou live, and thou shalt serve thy brother;
And it shall come to pass when thou shalt break loose,
That thou shalt shake his yoke from off thy neck.

(41) And Esau hated Jacob because of the blessing wherewith his father blessed him: and Esau said in his heart, The days of mourning for my father are at hand; then will I slay my brother Jacob. (42) And the words of Esau her elder son were told to Rebekah; and she sent and called Jacob her younger son, and said unto him, Behold, thy brother Esau, as touching thee, doth comfort himself, *purposing* to kill thee. (43) Now therefore, my son, obey my voice; and arise, flee thou to Laban my brother to Haran; (44) and tarry with him a few days, until thy brother's fury turn away; (45) until thy brother's anger turn away from thee, and he forget that which thou hast done to him: then I will send, and fetch thee from thence: why should I be bereaved of you both in one day?

(46) And Rebekah said to Isaac, I am weary of my life because of the daughters of Heth: if Jacob take a wife of the daughters of Heth, such as these daughters of the land, what good shall my life do me? **28** And Isaac called Jacob, and blessed him, and charged him, and said unto him, Thou shalt not take a wife of the daughters of Canaan. (2) Arise, go

---

¹ See ch. xxv. 26. ² Or, *away from*.

to Paddan-aram, to the house of Bethuel thy mother's father; and take thee a wife from thence of the daughters of Laban thy mother's brother. (3) And ¹God Almighty bless thee, and make thee fruitful, and multiply thee, that thou mayest be a company of peoples; (4) and give thee the blessing of Abraham, to thee, and to thy seed with thee; that thou mayest inherit the land of thy sojournings, which God gave unto Abraham. (5) And Isaac sent away Jacob: and he went to Paddan-aram unto Laban, son of Bethuel the ²Syrian, the brother of Rebekah, Jacob's and Esau's mother. (6) Now Esau saw that Isaac had blessed Jacob and sent him away to Paddan-aram, to take him a wife from thence; and that as he blessed him he gave him a charge, saying, Thou shalt not take a wife of the daughters of Canaan: (7) and that Jacob obeyed his father and his mother, and was gone to Paddan-aram: (8) and Esau saw that the daughters of Canaan pleased not Isaac his father; (9) and Esau went unto Ishmael, and took unto the wives which he had Mahalath the daughter of Ishmael Abraham's son, the sister of Nebaioth, to be his wife.

(10) And Jacob went out from Beer-sheba, and went toward Haran. (11) And he lighted upon ³a certain place, and tarried there all night, because the sun was set; and he took one of the stones of the place, and put it under his head, and lay down in that place to sleep. (12) And he dreamed, and behold a ladder set up on the earth, and the top of it reached to heaven: and behold the angels of God ascending and descending on it. (13) And, behold, the LORD stood ⁴above it, and said, I am the LORD, the God of Abraham thy father, and the God of Isaac: the land whereon thou liest, to thee will I give it, and to thy seed; (14) and thy seed shall be as the dust of the earth, and thou shalt ⁵spread abroad to the west, and to the east, and to the north, and to the south: and in thee and in thy seed shall all the families of the earth be blessed. (15) And, behold, I am with thee, and will keep thee whithersoever thou goest, and will bring thee again into this land; for I will not leave thee, until I have done that which I have spoken to thee of. (16) And Jacob awaked out of his sleep, and he said, Surely the LORD is in this place; and I knew it not. (17) And he was afraid, and said, How dreadful is this place! this is none other but the house of God, and this is the gate of heaven. (18) And Jacob rose up early in the morning, and took the stone that he had put under his head, and set it up for a pillar, and poured oil upon the top of it. (19) And he called the name of that place ⁶Beth-el: but the name of the city was Luz at the first. (20) And Jacob vowed a vow, saying, If God will be with me, and will keep me in this way that I go, and will give me bread to eat, and raiment to put on, (21) so that I come again to my father's house in peace, ⁷then shall the LORD be my God, (22) and this stone, which I have set up for a pillar, shall be God's house: and of all that thou shalt give me I will surely give the tenth unto thee.

29 Then Jacob ⁸went on his journey, and came to the land of the children of the east. (2) And he looked, and behold a well in the field, and, lo, three flocks of sheep lying there by it; for out of that well they watered the flocks: and the stone upon the well's mouth was great. (3) And thither were all the flocks gathered: and they rolled the stone from the well's mouth, and watered the sheep, and put the stone again upon the well's mouth in its place. (4) And Jacob said unto them, My brethren, whence be ye? And

---
¹ Heb. *El Shaddai*. ² Heb. *Aramean*. ³ Heb. *the place*. ⁴ Or, *beside him*. ⁵ Heb. *break forth*.
⁶ That is, *The house of God*. ⁷ Or, *and the LORD will be my God, then this stone &c.* ⁸ Heb. *lifted up his feet*.

they said, Of Haran are we. (5) And he said unto them, Know ye Laban the son of Nahor? And they said, We know him. (6) And he said unto them, Is it well with him? And they said, It is well: and, behold, Rachel his daughter cometh with the sheep. (7) And he said, Lo, it is yet high day, neither is it time that the cattle should be gathered together: water ye the sheep, and go and feed them. (8) And they said, We cannot, until all the flocks be gathered together, and they roll the stone from the well's mouth; then we water the sheep. (9) While he yet spake with them, Rachel came with her father's sheep; for she kept them. (10) And it came to pass, when Jacob saw Rachel the daughter of Laban his mother's brother, and the sheep of Laban his mother's brother, that Jacob went near, and rolled the stone from the well's mouth, and watered the flock of Laban his mother's brother. (11) And Jacob kissed Rachel, and lifted up his voice, and wept. (12) And Jacob told Rachel that he was her father's brother, and that he was Rebekah's son: and she ran and told her father. (13) And it came to pass, when Laban heard the tidings of Jacob his sister's son, that he ran to meet him, and embraced him, and kissed him, and brought him to his house. And he told Laban all these things. (14) And Laban said to him, Surely thou art my bone and my flesh. And he abode with him the space of a month. (15) And Laban said unto Jacob, Because thou art my brother, shouldest thou therefore serve me for nought? tell me, what shall thy wages be? (16) And Laban had two daughters: the name of the elder was Leah, and the name of the younger was Rachel. (17) And Leah's eyes were tender: but Rachel was beautiful and well favoured. (18) And Jacob loved Rachel; and he said, I will serve thee seven years for Rachel thy younger daughter. (19) And Laban said, It is better that I give her to thee, than that I should give her to another man: abide with me. (20) And Jacob served seven years for Rachel; and they seemed unto him but a few days, for the love he had to her. (21) And Jacob said unto Laban, Give me my wife, for my days are fulfilled, that I may go in unto her. (22) And Laban gathered together all the men of the place, and made a feast. (23) And it came to pass in the evening, that he took Leah his daughter, and brought her to him; and he went in unto her. (24) And Laban gave Zilpah his handmaid unto his daughter Leah for an handmaid. (25) And it came to pass in the morning, that, behold, it was Leah: and he said to Laban, What is this thou hast done unto me? did not I serve with thee for Rachel? wherefore then hast thou beguiled me? (26) And Laban said, It is not so done in our place, to give the younger before the firstborn. (27) Fulfil the week of this one, and we will give thee the other also for the service which thou shalt serve with me yet seven other years. (28) And Jacob did so, and fulfilled her week: and he gave him Rachel his daughter to wife. (29) And Laban gave to Rachel his daughter Bilhah his handmaid to be her handmaid. (30) And he went in also unto Rachel, and he loved also Rachel more than Leah, and served with him yet seven other years.

(31) And the LORD saw that Leah was hated, and he opened her womb: but Rachel was barren. (32) And Leah conceived, and bare a son, and she called his name Reuben: for she said, Because the LORD [1] hath looked upon my affliction; for now my husband will love me. (33) And she conceived again, and bare a son; and said, Because the LORD [2] hath heard that I am hated, he hath therefore given me this son also: and she called his name [3] Sim-

---

[1] Heb. *raah beonyi*.   [2] Heb. *shama*.   [3] Heb. *Shimeon*.

con. (34) And she conceived again, and bare a son; and said, Now this time will my husband be ¹joined unto me, because I have borne him three sons: therefore was his name called Levi. (35) And she conceived again, and bare a son; and she said, This time will I ²praise the LORD: therefore she called his name ³Judah; and she left bearing.

30 And when Rachel saw that she bare Jacob no children, Rachel envied her sister: and she said unto Jacob, Give me children, or else I die. (2) And Jacob's anger was kindled against Rachel: and he said, Am I in God's stead, who hath withheld from thee the fruit of the womb? (3) And she said, Behold my maid Bilhah, go in unto her; that she may bear upon my knees, and I also may ⁴obtain children by her. (4) And she gave him Bilhah her handmaid to wife: and Jacob went in unto her. (5) And Bilhah conceived, and bare Jacob a son. (6) And Rachel said, God hath ⁵judged me, and hath also heard my voice, and hath given me a son: therefore called she his name Dan. (7) And Bilhah Rachel's handmaid conceived again, and bare Jacob a second son. (8) And Rachel said, With ⁶mighty wrestlings have I ⁷wrestled with my sister, and have prevailed: and she called his name Naphtali. (9) When Leah saw that she had left bearing, she took Zilpah her handmaid, and gave her to Jacob to wife. (10) And Zilpah Leah's handmaid bare Jacob a son. (11) And Leah said, ⁸Fortunate! and she called his name ⁹Gad. (12) And Zilpah Leah's handmaid bare Jacob a second son. (13) And Leah said, ¹⁰Happy am I! for the daughters will ¹¹call me happy: and she called his name Asher. (14) And Reuben went in the days of wheat harvest, and found ¹²mandrakes in the field, and brought them unto his mother Leah.

Then Rachel said to Leah, Give me, I pray thee, of thy son's mandrakes. (15) And she said unto her, Is it a small matter that thou hast taken away my husband? and wouldest thou take away my son's mandrakes also? And Rachel said, Therefore he shall lie with thee to-night for thy son's mandrakes. (16) And Jacob came from the field in the evening, and Leah went out to meet him, and said, Thou must come in unto me; for I have surely hired thee with my son's mandrakes. And he lay with her that night. (17) And God hearkened unto Leah, and she conceived, and bare Jacob a fifth son. (18) And Leah said, God hath given me my ¹³hire, because I gave my handmaid to my husband: and she called his name Issachar. (19) And Leah conceived again, and bare a sixth son to Jacob. (20) And Leah said, God hath endowed me with a good dowry now will my husband ¹⁴dwell with me, because I have borne him six sons: and she called his name Zebulun. (21) And afterwards she bare a daughter, and called her name Dinah. (22) And God remembered Rachel, and God hearkened to her, and opened her womb. (23) And she conceived, and bare a son; and said, God hath taken away my reproach: (24) and she called his name Joseph, saying, The LORD ¹⁵add to me another son.

(25) And it came to pass, when Rachel had borne Joseph, that Jacob said unto Laban, Send me away, that I may go unto mine own place, and to my country. (26) Give me my wives and my children for whom I have served thee, and let me go: for thou knowest my service wherewith I have served thee. (27) And Laban said unto him, If now I have found favour in thine eyes, *tarry: for* I have divined that the LORD hath blessed me for thy sake. (28) And he said, Appoint me thy wages.

---

¹ From the root *larah*. ² From the Heb. *hodah*. ³ Heb. *Jehudah*. ⁴ Heb. *be builded by her*. ⁵ Heb. *dan*, he judged. ⁶ Heb. *wrestlings of God*. ⁷ Heb. *niphtal*, he wrestled. ⁸ Heb. *With fortune!* Another reading is, *Fortune is come*. ⁹ That is, *Fortune*. ¹⁰ Heb. *With my happiness!* ¹¹ Heb. *asher*, to call happy. ¹² Or, *love-apples*. ¹³ Heb. *sachar*. ¹⁴ Heb. *zabal*, he dwelt. ¹⁵ Heb. *joseph*.

# GENESIS.

and I will give it. (29) And he said unto him, Thou knowest how I have served thee, and how thy cattle hath fared with me. (30) For it was little which thou hadst before I came, and it hath ¹increased unto a multitude: and the LORD hath blessed thee ² whithersoever I turned: and now when shall I provide for mine own house also? (31) And he said, What shall I give thee? And Jacob said, Thou shalt not give me aught: if thou wilt do this thing for me, I will again feed thy flock and keep it. (32) I will pass through all thy flock to-day, removing from thence every speckled and spotted one, and every black one among the sheep, and the spotted and speckled among the goats: and of such shall be my hire. (33) So shall my righteousness answer for me hereafter, when thou shalt come concerning my hire that is before thee: every one that is not speckled and spotted among the goats, and black among the sheep, that if found with me shall be counted stolen. (34) And Laban said, Behold, I would it might be according to thy word. (35) And he removed that day the he-goats that were ringstraked and spotted, and all the she-goats that were speckled and spotted, every one that had white in it, and all the black ones among the sheep, and gave them into the hand of his sons; (36) and he set three days' journey betwixt himself and Jacob: and Jacob fed the rest of Laban's flocks. (37) And Jacob took him rods of fresh ³poplar, and of the almond and of the plane tree; and peeled white strakes in them, and made the white appear which was in the rods. (38) And he set the rods which he had peeled over against the flocks in the gutters in the watering troughs where the flocks came to drink; and they conceived when they came to drink. (39) And the flocks conceived before the rods, and the flocks brought forth ringstraked, speckled, and spotted. (40) And Jacob separated the lambs, and set the faces of the flocks toward the ringstraked and all the black in the flock of Laban; and he put his own droves apart, and put them not unto Laban's flock. (41) And it came to pass, whensoever the stronger of the flock did conceive, that Jacob laid the rods before the eyes of the flock in the gutters, that they might conceive among the rods; (42) but when the flock were feeble, he put them not in: so the feebler were Laban's, and the stronger Jacob's. (43) And the man increased exceedingly, and had large flocks, and maidservants and menservants, and camels and asses.

31 And he heard the words of Laban's sons, saying, Jacob hath taken away all that was our father's; and of that which was our father's hath he gotten all this ⁴glory. (2) And Jacob beheld the countenance of Laban, and, behold, it was not toward him as beforetime. (3) And the LORD said unto Jacob, Return unto the land of thy fathers, and to thy kindred; and I will be with thee. (4) And Jacob sent and called Rachel and Leah to the field unto his flock, (5) and said unto them, I see your father's countenance, that it is not toward me as beforetime: but the God of my father hath been with me. (6) And ye know that with all my power I have served your father. (7) And your father hath deceived me, and changed my wages ten times; but God suffered him not to hurt me. (8) If he said thus, The speckled shall be thy wages; then all the flock bare speckled: and if he said thus, The ringstraked shall be thy wages; then bare all the flock ringstraked. (9) Thus God hath taken away the cattle of your father, and given them to me. (10) And it came to pass at the time that the flock conceived, that I lifted up mine eyes, and saw in a dream, and, behold, the he-goats which leaped upon the flock were ring-

¹ Heb. *broken forth.*   ² Heb. *at my foot.*   ³ Or, *storax tree.*   ⁴ Or, *wealth.*

straked, speckled, and grisled. (11) And the angel of God said unto me in the dream, Jacob: and I said, Here am I. (12) And he said, Lift up now thine eyes, and see, all the he-goats which leap upon the flock are ringstraked, speckled, and grisled: *for I have seen all that Laban doeth unto thee.* (13) I am the God of Beth-el, where thou anointedst a pillar, where thou vowedst a vow unto me: now arise, get thee out from this land, and return unto the land of thy nativity. (14) And Rachel and Leah answered and said unto him, Is there yet any portion or inheritance for us in our father's house? (15) Are we not counted of him strangers? for he hath sold us, and hath also quite devoured [1] our money. (16) For all the riches which God hath taken away from our father, that is ours and our children's: now then, whatsoever God hath said unto thee, do. (17) Then Jacob rose up, and set his sons and his wives upon the camels; (18) and he carried away all his cattle, **and all his substance which he had gathered, the cattle of his getting, which he had gathered in Paddan-aram, for to go to Isaac his father unto the land of Canaan.** (19) Now Laban was gone to shear his sheep: and Rachel stole the [2] teraphim that were her father's. (20) And Jacob [3] stole away unawares to Laban the Syrian, in that he told him not that he fled. (21) So he fled with all that he had; **and he rose up, and passed over** [4] **the River,** and set his face toward the mountain of Gilead.

(22) And it was told Laban on the third day that Jacob was fled. (23) And he took his brethren with him, and pursued after him seven days' journey; and he overtook him in the mountain of Gilead. (24) And God came to Laban the Syrian in a dream of the night, and said unto him, Take heed to thyself that thou speak not to Jacob either good or bad. (25) And Laban came up with Jacob. Now Jacob had pitched his tent in the mountain: and Laban with his brethren pitched in the mountain of Gilead. (26) And Laban said to Jacob, What hast thou done, that thou hast stolen away unawares to me, and carried away my daughters as captives of the sword? (27) **Wherefore didst thou flee secretly, and** [5] **steal away from me; and didst not tell me, that I might have sent thee away with mirth and with songs, with tabret and with harp;** (28) and hast not suffered me to kiss my sons and my daughters? now hast thou done foolishly. (29) It is in the power of my hand to do you hurt: but the God of your father spake unto me yesternight, saying, Take heed to thyself that thou speak not to Jacob either good or bad. (30) And now, *though* thou wouldest needs be gone, because thou sore longedst after thy father's house, *yet* wherefore hast thou stolen my gods? (31) And Jacob answered and said to Laban, Because I was afraid: for I said, Lest thou shouldest take thy daughters from me by force. (32) With whomsoever thou findest thy gods, he shall not live: before our brethren discern thou what is thine with me, and take it to thee. For Jacob knew not that Rachel had stolen them. (33) And Laban went into Jacob's tent, and into Leah's tent, and into the tent of the two maidservants; but he found them not. And he went out of Leah's tent, and entered into Rachel's tent. (34) Now Rachel had taken the teraphim, and put them in the camel's furniture, and sat upon them. And Laban felt about all the tent, but found them not. (35) And she said to her father, Let not my lord be angry that I cannot rise up before thee; for the manner of women is upon me. And he searched, but found not the teraphim.

---

[1] Or, *the price paid for us.*   [2] See vv. 30, 34, Judg. xvii. 5, 1 Sam. xix. 13, and Hos. iii. 4.   [3] Heb. *stole the heart of Laban the Aramean.*   [4] That is, the Euphrates.   [5] Heb. *didst steal me.*

(36) And Jacob was wroth, and chode with Laban: and Jacob answered and said to Laban, What is my trespass? what is my sin, that thou hast hotly pursued after me? (37) Whereas thou hast felt about all my stuff, what hast thou found of all thy household stuff? Set it here before my brethren and thy brethren, that they may judge betwixt us two. (38) This twenty years have I been with thee; thy ewes and thy she-goats have not cast their young, and the rams of thy flocks have I not eaten. (39) That which was torn of beasts I brought not unto thee; I bare the loss of it: of my hand didst thou require it, whether stolen by day or stolen by night. (40) Thus I was; in the day the drought consumed me, and the frost by night; and my sleep fled from mine eyes. (41) These twenty years have I been in thy house; I served thee fourteen years for thy two daughters, and six years for thy flock: and thou hast changed my wages ten times. (42) Except the God of my father, the God of Abraham, and the Fear of Isaac, had been with me, surely now hadst thou sent me away empty. God hath seen mine affliction and the labour of my hands, and rebuked thee yesternight. (43) And Laban answered and said unto Jacob, The daughters are my daughters, and the children are my children, and the flocks are my flocks, and all that thou seest is mine: and what can I do this day unto these my daughters, or unto their children which they have borne? (44) And now come, let us make a covenant, I and thou; and let it be for a witness between me and thee. (45) And Jacob took a stone, and set it up for a pillar. (46) And Jacob said unto his brethren, Gather stones; and they took stones, and made an heap: and they did eat there by the heap. (47) And Laban called it ¹Jegar-sahadutha: but Jacob called it ²Galeed. (48) And Laban said, This heap is witness between me and thee this day. Therefore was the name of it called Galeed: (49) and Mizpah, for he said, The LORD watch between me and thee, when we are ⁴absent one from another. (50) If thou shalt afflict my daughters, and if thou shalt take wives beside my daughters, no man is with us; see, God is witness betwixt me and thee. (51) And Laban said to Jacob, Behold this heap, and behold the pillar, which I have set betwixt me and thee. (52) This heap be witness, and the pillar be witness, that I will not pass over this heap to thee, and that thou shalt not pass over this heap and this pillar unto me, for harm. (53) The God of Abraham, and the God of Nahor, the ⁵God of their father, judge betwixt us. And Jacob sware by the Fear of his father Isaac. (54) And Jacob offered a sacrifice in the mountain, and called his brethren to eat bread: and they did eat bread, and tarried all night in the mountain. (55) ⁶And early in the morning Laban rose up, and kissed his sons and his daughters, and blessed them: and Laban departed, and returned unto his place. **32** And Jacob went on his way, and the angels of God met him. (2) And Jacob said when he saw them, This is God's host: and he called the name of that place ⁷Mahanaim.

(3) And Jacob sent messengers before him to Esau his brother unto the land of Seir, the field of Edom. (4) And he commanded them, saying, Thus shall ye say unto my lord Esau; Thus saith thy servant Jacob, I have sojourned with Laban, and stayed until now: (5) and I have oxen, and asses *and* flocks, and menservants and maidservants: and I have sent to tell my lord, that I may find grace in thy sight. (6) And the messengers returned to Jacob, saying, We came to thy

---
¹ That is, *The heap of witness*, in Aramaic.   ² That is, *The heap of witness*, in Hebrew.   ³ That is, *The watchtower*.   ⁴ Heb. *hidden*.   ⁵ Or, *gods*.   ⁶ In Heb. ch. xxxii. begins here.   ⁷ That is, *Hosts*, or, *Companies*.

brother Esau, and moreover he cometh to meet thee, and four hundred men with him. (7) Then Jacob was greatly afraid and was distressed: and he divided the people that was with him, and the flocks, and the herds, and the camels, into two companies; (8) and he said, If Esau come to the one company, and smite it, then the company which is left shall escape. (9) And Jacob said, O God of my father Abraham, and God of my father Isaac, O LORD, which saidst unto me, Return unto thy country, and to thy kindred, and I will do thee good: (10) [1] I am not worthy of the least of all the mercies, and of all the truth, which thou hast shewed unto thy servant; for with my staff I passed over this Jordan; and now I am become two companies. (11) Deliver me, I pray thee, from the hand of my brother, from the hand of Esau: for I fear him, lest he come and smite me, the mother with the children. (12) And thou saidst, I will surely do thee good, and make thy seed as the sand of the sea, which cannot be numbered for multitude. (13) And he lodged there that night; and took of that which he had with him a present for Esau his brother; (14) two hundred she-goats and twenty he-goats, two hundred ewes and twenty rams, (15) thirty milch camels and their colts, forty kine and ten bulls, twenty she-asses and ten foals. (16) And he delivered them into the hand of his servants, every drove by itself; and said unto his servants, Pass over before me, and put a space betwixt drove and drove. (17) And he commanded the foremost, saying, When Esau my brother meeteth thee, and asketh thee, saying, Whose art thou? and whither goest thou? and whose are these before thee? (18) then thou shalt say, They be thy servant Jacob's; it is a present sent unto my lord Esau: and, behold, he also is behind us. (19) And he commanded also the second, and the third, and all that followed the droves, saying, On this manner shall ye speak unto Esau, when ye find him; (20) and ye shall say, Moreover, behold, thy servant Jacob is behind us. For he said, I will appease him with the present that goeth before me, and afterward I will see his face; peradventure he will accept me. (21) So the present passed over before him: and he himself lodged that night in the company.

(22) And he rose up that night, and took his two wives, and his two handmaids, and his eleven children, and passed over the ford of Jabbok. (23) And he took them, and sent them over the stream, and sent over that he had. (24) And Jacob was left alone; and there wrestled a man with him until the breaking of the day. (25) And when he saw that he prevailed not against him, he touched the hollow of his thigh; and the hollow of Jacob's thigh was strained, as he wrestled with him. (26) And he said, Let me go, for the day breaketh. And he said, I will not let thee go, except thou bless me. (27) And he said unto him, What is thy name? And he said, Jacob. (28) And he said, Thy name shall be called no more Jacob, but [2] Israel: for [3] thou hast [4] striven with God and *with* men, and hast prevailed. (29) And Jacob asked him, and said, Tell me, I pray thee, thy name. And he said, Wherefore is it that thou dost ask after my name? And he blessed him there. (30) And Jacob called the name of the place [5] Peniel: for, *said he*, I have seen God face to face, and my life is preserved. (31) And the sun rose upon him as he passed over Penuel, and he halted upon his thigh. (32) Therefore the children of Israel eat not the sinew of the hip which is upon the hollow of the thigh, unto this day: because he touched the hollow of Jacob's thigh in the sinew of the hip.

---

[1] Heb. *I am less than all &c.* [2] That is, *He who striveth with God*, or, *God striveth*. [3] The Sept. and Vulgate have, *thou hast had power with God, and thou shalt prevail against men.* [4] Or, *had power with.* [5] That is, *The face of God.*

33 And Jacob lifted up his eyes, and looked, and, behold, Esau came, and with him four hundred men. And he divided the children unto Leah, and unto Rachel, and unto the two handmaids. (2) And he put the handmaids and their children foremost, and Leah and her children after, and Rachel and Joseph hindermost. (3) And he himself passed over before them, and bowed himself to the ground seven times, until he came near to his brother. (4) And Esau ran to meet him, and embraced him, and fell on his neck, and kissed him: and they wept. (5) And he lifted up his eyes, and saw the women and the children; and said, Who are these with thee? And he said, The children which God hath graciously given thy servant. (6) Then the handmaids came near, they and their children, and they bowed themselves. (7) And Leah also and her children came near, and bowed themselves: and after came Joseph near and Rachel, and they bowed themselves. (8) And he said, What meanest thou by all this company which I met? And he said, To find grace in the sight of my lord. (9) And Esau said, I have enough; my brother, let that thou hast be thine. (10) And Jacob said, Nay, I pray thee, if now I have found grace in thy sight, then receive my present at my hand: ¹forasmuch as I have seen thy face, as one seeth the face of God, and thou wast pleased with me. (11) Take, I pray thee, my ²gift that is brought to thee; because God hath dealt graciously with me, and because I have ³enough. And he urged him, and he took it. (12) And he said, Let us take our journey, and let us go, and I will go before thee. (13) And he said unto him, My lord knoweth that the children are tender, and that the flocks and herds with me give suck: and if they overdrive them one day, all the flocks will die. (14) Let my lord, I pray thee, pass over before his servant: and I will lead on softly, according to the pace of the cattle that is before me and according to the pace of the children, until I come unto my lord unto Seir. (15) And Esau said, Let me now leave with thee some of the folk that are with me. And he said, What needeth it? let me find grace in the sight of my lord. (16) So Esau returned that day on his way unto Seir. (17) And Jacob journeyed to Succoth, and built him an house, and made booths for his cattle: therefore the name of the place is called ⁴Succoth.

(18) And Jacob came ⁵in peace to the city of Shechem, which is in the land of Canaan, when he came from Paddan-aram; and encamped before the city. (19) And he bought the parcel of ground, where he had spread his tent, at the hand of the children of Hamor, Shechem's father, for an hundred ⁶pieces of money. (20) And he erected there an altar, and called it ⁷El-elohe-Israel.

34 And Dinah the daughter of Leah, which she bare unto Jacob, went out to see the daughters of the land. (2) And Shechem the son of Hamor the Hivite, the prince of the land, saw her; and he took her, and lay with her, and humbled her. (3) And his soul clave unto Dinah the daughter of Jacob, and he loved the damsel, and spake kindly unto the damsel. (4) And Shechem spake unto his father Hamor, saying, Get me this damsel to wife. (5) Now Jacob heard that he had defiled Dinah his daughter; and his sons were with his cattle in the field: and Jacob held his peace until they came. (6) And Hamor the father of Shechem went out unto Jacob to commune with him. (7) And the sons of Jacob came in from the field when they heard it: and the men were grieved, and they were very wroth, because he had wrought folly in Israel in lying with Ja-

---
¹ Or, *for therefore have I seen.* ² Heb. *blessing.* ³ Heb. *all.* ⁴ That is, *Booth s.* ⁵ Or, *to Shalem, a city.*
⁶ Heb. *kesitah.* ⁷ That is, *God, the God of Israel.* ⁸ Heb. *to the heart of the damsel.*

cob's daughter; which thing ought not to be done. (8) And Hamor communed with them, saying. The soul of my son Shechem longeth for your daughter: I pray you give her unto him to wife. (9) And make ye marriages with us; give your daughters unto us, and take our daughters unto you. (10) And ye shall dwell with us: and the land shall be before you; dwell and trade ye therein, and get you possessions therein. (11) And Shechem said unto her father and unto her brethren, Let me find grace in your eyes, and what ye shall say unto me I will give. (12) Ask me never so much dowry and gift, and I will give according as ye shall say unto me: but give me the damsel to wife. (13) And the sons of Jacob answered Shechem and Hamor his father with guile, and spake, because he had defiled Dinah their sister, (14) and said unto them. We cannot do this thing, to give our sister to one that is uncircumcised: for that were a reproach unto us: (15) only on this condition will we consent unto you: if ye will be as we be, that every male of you be circumcised; (16) then will we give our daughters unto you, and we will take your daughters to us, and we will dwell with you, and we will become one people. (17) But if ye will not hearken unto us, to be circumcised; then will we take our daughter, and we will be gone. (18) And their words pleased Hamor, and Shechem Hamor's son. (19) And the young man deferred not to do the thing, because he had delight in Jacob's daughter: and he was honoured above all the house of his father. (20) And Hamor and Shechem his son came unto the gate of their city, and communed with the men of their city, saying. (21) These men are peaceable with us; therefore let them dwell in the land, and trade therein; for, behold, the land is large enough for them: let us take their daughters to us for wives, and let us give them our daughters. (22) Only on this condition will the men consent unto us to dwell with us, to become one people, if every male among us be circumcised, as they are circumcised. (23) Shall not their cattle and their substance and all their beasts be ours? only let us consent unto them, and they will dwell with us. (24) And unto Hamor and unto Shechem his son hearkened all that went out of the gate of his city: and every male was circumcised, all that went out of the gate of his city. (25) And it came to pass on the third day, when they were sore, that two of the sons of Jacob, Simeon and Levi, Dinah's brethren, took each man his sword, and came upon the city [1] unawares, and slew all the males. (26) And they slew Hamor and Shechem his son with the edge of the sword, and took Dinah out of Shechem's house, and went forth. (27) The sons of Jacob came upon the slain, and spoiled the city, because they had defiled their sister. (28) They took their flocks and their herds and their asses, and that which was in the city, and that which was in the field; (29) and all their wealth, and all their little ones and their wives, took they captive and spoiled, even all that was in the house. (30) And Jacob said to Simeon and Levi, Ye have troubled me, to make me to stink among the inhabitants of the land, among the Canaanites and the Perizzites: and, I being few in number, they will gather themselves together against me and smite me; and I shall be destroyed, I and my house. (31) And they said, Should he deal with our sister as with an harlot?

35 And God said unto Jacob, Arise, go up to Beth-el, and dwell there: and make there an altar unto God, who appeared unto thee when thou fleddest from the face of Esau thy brother. (2) Then Jacob said unto his household, and to all that were with him, Put away the strange gods that are among you, and purify your-

---
[1] Or, *boldly.*

selves, and change your garments: (3) and let us arise, and go up to Beth-el; and I will make there an altar unto God, who answered me in the day of my distress, and was with me in the way which I went. (4) And they gave unto Jacob all the strange gods which were in their hand, and the rings which were in their ears; and Jacob hid them under the ¹oak which was by Shechem. (5) And they journeyed: and ²a great terror was upon the cities that were round about them, and they did not pursue after the sons of Jacob. (6) So Jacob came to Luz, which is in the land of Canaan (the same is Beth-el), he and all the people that were with him. (7) And he built there an altar, and called the place ³El-beth-el: because there God was revealed unto him, when he fled from the face of his brother. (8) And Deborah Rebekah's nurse died, and she was buried below Beth-el under the oak: and the name of it was called ⁴Allon-bacuth.

(9) And God appeared unto Jacob again, when he came from Paddan-aram, and blessed him. (10) And God said unto him, Thy name is Jacob: thy name shall not be called any more Jacob, but Israel shall be thy name: and he called his name Israel. (11) And God said unto him, I am ⁵God Almighty: be fruitful and multiply; a nation and a company of nations shall be of thee, and kings shall come out of thy loins; (12) and the land which I gave unto Abraham and Isaac, to thee I will give it, and to thy seed after thee will I give the land. (13) And God went up from him in the place where he spake with him. (14) And Jacob set up a pillar in the place where he spake with him, a pillar of stone: and he poured out a drink offering thereon, and poured oil thereon. (15) And Jacob called the name of the place where God spake with him, Beth-el. (16) And they journeyed from Beth-el; and there was still some way to come to Ephrath: and Rachel travailed, and she had hard labour. (17) And it came to pass, when she was in hard labour, that the midwife said unto her, Fear not; for now thou shalt have another son. (18) And it came to pass, as her soul was in departing (for she died), that she called his name ⁶Ben-oni: but his father called him ⁷Benjamin. (19) And Rachel died, and was buried in the way to Ephrath (the same is Beth-lehem). (20) And Jacob set up a pillar upon her grave: the same is the Pillar of Rachel's grave unto this day. (21) And Israel journeyed, and spread his tent beyond the tower of Eder. (22) And it came to pass, while Israel dwelt in that land, that Reuben went and lay with Bilhah his father's concubine: and Israel heard of it.

Now the sons of Jacob were twelve: (23) the sons of Leah; Reuben, Jacob's firstborn, and Simeon, and Levi, and Judah, and Issachar, and Zebulun: (24) the sons of Rachel: Joseph and Benjamin: (25) and the sons of Bilhah, Rachel's handmaid; Dan and Naphtali: (26) and the sons of Zilpah, Leah's handmaid; Gad and Asher: these are the sons of Jacob, which were born to him in Paddan-aram. (27) And Jacob came unto Isaac his father to Mamre, to Kiriatharba (the same is Hebron), where Abraham and Isaac sojourned. (28) And the days of Isaac were an hundred and fourscore years. (29) And Isaac gave up the ghost, and died, and was gathered unto his people, old and full of days: and Esau and Jacob his sons buried him.

36 Now these are the generations of Esau (the same is Edom). (2) Esau took his wives of the daughters of Canaan; Adah the daughter of Elon the Hittite,

---
¹ Or, *terebinth*. ² Heb. *a terror of God*. ³ That is, *The God of Beth-el*. ⁴ That is, *The oak of weeping*. ⁵ Heb *El Shaddai*. ⁶ That is, *The son of my sorrow*. ⁷ That is, *The son of the right hand*.

GENESIS.

and Oiolibamah the daughter of Anah the daughter of Zibeon the Hivite; (3) and Basemath Ishmael's daughter, sister of Nebaioth. (4) And Adah bare to Esau Eliphaz; and Basemath bare Reuel; and Oholibamah bare Jeush, and Jalam, and Korah: these are the sons of Esau, which were born unto him in the land of Canaan. (6) **And Esau took his wives, and his sons, and his daughters, and all the souls of his house, and his cattle, and all his beasts, and all his possessions, which he had gathered in the land of Canaan; and went into a land away from his brother Jacob.** (7) For their substance was too great for them to dwell together; and the land of their sojournings could not bear them because of their cattle. (8) **And Esau dwelt in mount Seir: Esau is Edom.** (9) And these are the generations of Esau the father of [2] the Edomites in mount Seir: (10) these are the names of Esau's sons; Eliphaz the son of Adah the wife of Esau, Reuel the son of Basemath the wife of Esau. (11) And the sons of Eliphaz were Teman, Omar, [3] Zepho, and Gatam, and Kenaz. (12) And Timna was concubine to Eliphaz Esau's son: and she bare to Eliphaz Amalek: these are the sons of Adah Esau's wife. (13) And these are the sons of Reuel: Nahath, and Zerah, Shammah, and Mizzah: these were the sons of Basemath Esau's wife. (14) And these were the sons of Oholibamah the daughter of Anah, the daughter of Zibeon, Esau's wife: and she bare to Esau Jeush, and Jalam, and Korah. (15) These are the [4] dukes of the sons of Esau: the sons of Eliphaz the firstborn of Esau; duke Teman, duke Omar, duke Zepho, duke Kenaz, (16) duke Korah, duke Gatam, duke Amalek: these are the dukes that came of Eliphaz in the land of Edom; these are the sons of Adah. (17) And these are the sons of Reuel Esau's son; duke Nahath, duke Zerah, duke Shammah, duke Mizzah: these are the dukes that came of Reuel in the land of Edom: these are the sons of Basemath Esau's wife. (18) And these are the sons of Oholibamah Esau's wife; duke Jeush, duke Jalam, duke Korah: these are the dukes that came of Oholibamah the daughter of Anah, Esau's wife. (19) These are the sons of Esau, and these are their dukes: the same is Edom.

(20) These are the sons of Seir the Horite, the inhabitants of the land; Lotan and Shobal and Zibeon and Anah, (21) and Dishon and Ezer and Dishan: these are the dukes that came of the Horites, the children of Seir in the land of Edom. (22) And the children of Lotan were Hori and [6] Hemam; and Lotan's sister was Timna. (23) And these are the children of Shobal; [6] Alvan and Manahath and Ebal, [7] Shepho and Onam. (24) And these are the children of Zibeon; Aiah and Anah: this is Anah who found the hot springs in the wilderness, as he fed the asses of Zibeon his father. (25) And these are the children of Anah; Dishon and Oholibamah the daughter of Anah. (26) And these are the children of [8] Dishon; [9] Hemdan and Eshban and Ithran and Cheran. (27) These are the children of Ezer; Bilhan and Zaavan and [10] Akan. (28) These are the children of Dishan; Uz and Aran. (29) These are the dukes that came of the Horites; duke Lotan, duke Shobal, duke Zibeon, duke Anah, (30) duke Dishon, duke Ezer, duke Dishan: these are the dukes that came of the Horites, according to their dukes in the land of Seir.

(31) **And these are the kings that reigned in the land of Edom, before there reigned any king over the children of Israel.** (32) And Bela the son of Beor

---
[1] Some ancient authorities have, *son*. See ver. 24.   [2] Heb. *Edom*.   [3] In 1 Chr. 1. 36, *Zephi*.   [4] Or, *chiefs*.
[5] In 1 Chr. 1. 39, *Homam*.   [6] In 1 Chr. 1. 40, *Alian*.   [7] In 1 Chr. 1. 40, *Shephi*.   [8] Heb. *Dishan*.   [9] In 1 Chr. 1. 41, *Hamran*.   [10] In 1 Chr. 1. 42, *Jaakan*.

reigned in Edom; and the name of his city was Dinhabah. (33) And Bela died, and Jobab the son of Zerah of Bozrah reigned in his stead. (34) And Jobab died, and Husham of the land of the Temanites reigned in his stead. (35) And Husham died, and Hadad the son of Bedad, who smote Midian in the field of Moab, reigned in his stead: and the name of his city was Avith. (36) And Hadad died, and Samlah of Masrekah reigned in his stead. (37) And Samlah died, and Shaul of Rehoboth by the River reigned in his stead. (38) And Shaul died, and Baal-hanan the son of Achbor reigned in his stead. (39) And Baal-hanan the son of Achbor died, and ¹Hadar reigned in his stead: and the name of his city was ²Pau; and his wife's name was Mehetabel, the daughter of Matred, the daughter of Me-zahab. (40) And these are the names of the dukes that came of Esau, according to their families, after their places, by their names; duke Timnah, duke ³Alvah, duke Jetheth; (41) duke Oholibamah, duke Elah, duke Pinon; (42) duke Kenaz, duke Teman, duke Mibzar; (43) duke Magdiel, duke Iram: these be the dukes of Edom, according to their habitations in the land of their possession. This is Esau the father of ⁴the Edomites.

37 And Jacob dwelt in the land of his father's sojournings, in the land of Canaan. (2) These are the generations of Jacob. Joseph, being seventeen years old, was feeding the flock with his brethren; and he was a lad with the sons of Bilhah, and with the sons of Zilpah, his father's wives: and Joseph brought the evil report of them unto their father. (3) Now Israel loved Joseph more than all his children, because he was the son of his old age: and he made him ⁵ a coat of many colours. (4) And his brethren saw that their father loved him more than all his brethren; and they hated him, and could not speak peaceably unto him. (5) And Joseph dreamed a dream, and he told it to his brethren: and they hated him yet the more. (6) And he said unto them, Hear, I pray you, this dream which I have dreamed: (7) for, behold, we were binding sheaves in the field, and, lo, my sheaf arose, and also stood upright; and, behold, your sheaves came round about, and made obeisance to my sheaf. (8) And his brethren said to him, Shalt thou indeed reign over us? or shalt thou indeed have dominion over us? And they hated him yet the more for his dreams, and for his words. (9) And he dreamed yet another dream, and told it to his brethren, and said, Behold, I have dreamed yet a dream; and, behold, the sun and the moon and eleven stars made obeisance to me. (10) And he told it to his father, and to his brethren; and his father rebuked him, and said unto him, What is this dream that thou hast dreamed? Shall I and thy mother and thy brethren indeed come to bow down ourselves to thee to the earth? (11) And his brethren envied him; but his father kept the saying in mind. (12) And his brethren went to feed their father's flock in Shechem. (13) And Israel said unto Joseph, Do not thy brethren feed the flock in Shechem? come, and I will send thee unto them. And he said to him, Here am I. (14) And he said to him, Go now, see whether it be well with thy brethren, and well with the flock; and bring me word again. So he sent him out of the vale of Hebron, and he came to Shechem. (15) And a certain man found him, and, behold, he was wandering in the field: and the man asked him, saying, What seekest thou? (16) And he said, I seek my brethren: tell me, I pray thee, where they are feeding *the flock*. (17) And the man said, They are departed

---

¹ In 1 Chr. l. 50, and some ancient authorities, *Hadad*. Edom. ² In 1 Chr. l. 50, *Pai*. ³ In 1 Chr. l. 51, *Aliah*. ⁴ Heb.
⁵ Or, *a long garment with sleeves*.

hence: for I heard them say, Let us go to Dothan. And Joseph went after his brethren, and found them in Dothan. (18) And they saw him afar off, and before he came near unto them, they conspired against him to slay him. (19) And they said one to another, Behold, this ¹ dreamer cometh. (20) Come now therefore, and let us slay him, and cast him into one of the pits, and we will say, An evil beast hath devoured him: and we shall see what will become of his dreams. (21) And Reuben heard it, and delivered him out of their hand; and said, Let us not take his life. (22) And Reuben said unto them, Shed no blood: cast him into this pit that is in the wilderness, but lay no hand upon him: that he might deliver him out of their hand, to restore him to his father. (23) And it came to pass, when Joseph was come unto his brethren, that they stript Joseph of his coat, the coat of many colours that was on him; (24) and they took him, and cast him into the pit: and the pit was empty, there was no water in it. (25) And they sat down to eat bread: and they lifted up their eyes and looked, and, behold, a travelling company of Ishmaelites came from Gilead, with their camels bearing ² spicery and ³ balm and ⁴ myrrh, going to carry it down to Egypt. (26) And Judah said unto his brethren, What profit is it if we slay our brother and conceal his blood? (27) Come, and let us sell him to the Ishmaelites, and let not our hand be upon him; for he is our brother, our flesh. And his brethren hearkened unto him. (28) And there passed by Midianites, merchantmen; and they drew and lifted up Joseph out of the pit, and sold Joseph to the Ishmaelites for twenty pieces of silver. And they brought Joseph into Egypt. (29) And Reuben returned unto the pit; and, behold, Joseph was not in the pit: and he rent his clothes. (30) And he returned unto his brethren, and said, The child is not; and I, whither shall I go? (31) And they took Joseph's coat, and killed a he-goat, and dipped the coat in the blood; (32) and they sent the coat of many colours, and they brought it to their father; and said, This have we found; know now whether it be thy son's coat or not. (33) And he knew it, and said, It is my son's coat; an evil beast hath devoured him; Joseph is without doubt torn in pieces. (34) And Jacob rent his garments, and put sackcloth upon his loins, and mourned for his son many days. (35) And all his sons and all his daughters rose up to comfort him; but he refused to be comforted; and he said, For I will go down to ⁶ the grave to my son mourning. And his father wept for him. (36) And the ⁶ Midianites sold him into Egypt unto Potiphar, an officer of Pharaoh's, the ⁷ captain of the guard.

38 And it came to pass at that time, that Judah went down from his brethren, and turned in to a certain Adullamite, whose name was Hirah. (2) And Judah saw there a daughter of a certain Canaanite whose name was Shua; and he took her, and went in unto her. (3) And she conceived, and bare a son; and he called his name Er. (4) And she conceived again, and bare a son; and she called his name Onan. (5) And she yet again bare a son, and called his name Shelah: and he was at Chezib, when she bare him. (6) And Judah took a wife for Er his firstborn, and her name was Tamar. (7) And Er, Judah's firstborn, was wicked in the sight of the LORD; and the LORD slew him. (8) And Judah said unto Onan, Go in unto thy brother's wife, and ⁸ perform the duty of an husband's brother unto her, and raise up seed to thy brother. (9) And Onan knew that the

---

¹ Heb. *master of dreams*. ² Or, *gum tragacanth*. Or, *storax*. ³ Or, *mastic*. ⁴ Or, *ladanum*. ⁵ Heb. *Sheol*, the name of the abode of the dead, answering to the Greek Hades, Acts ii. 27. ⁶ Heb. *Medanites*. ⁷ Heb. *chief of the executioners*. ⁸ See Deut. xxv. 5.

GENESIS. 43

seed should not be his; and it came to pass, when he went in unto his brother's wife, that he spilled it on the ground, lest he should give seed to his brother. (10) And the thing which he did was evil in the sight of the LORD: and he slew him also. (11) Then said Judah to Tamar his daughter in law, Remain a widow in thy father's house, till Shelah my son be grown up: for he said, Lest he also die, like his brethren. And Tamar went and dwelt in her father's house. (12) And in process of time Shua's daughter, the wife of Judah, died; and Judah was comforted, and went up unto his sheepshearers to Timnah, he and his friend Hirah the Adullamite. (13) And it was told Tamar, saying, Behold, thy father in law goeth up to Timnah to shear his sheep. (14) And she put off from her the garments of her widowhood, and covered herself with her veil, and wrapped herself, and sat in the gate of Enaim, which is by the way to Timnah; for she saw that Shelah was grown up, and she was not given unto him to wife. (15) When Judah saw her, he thought her to be an harlot; for she had covered her face. (16) And he turned unto her by the way, and said, Go to, I pray thee, let me come in unto thee: for he knew not that she was his daughter in law. And she said, What wilt thou give me, that thou mayest come in unto me? (17) And he said, I will send thee a kid of the goats from the flock. And she said, Wilt thou give me a pledge, till thou send it? (18) And he said, What pledge shall I give thee? And she said, Thy signet and thy cord, and thy staff that is in thine hand. And he gave them to her, and came in unto her, and she conceived by him. (19) And she arose, and went away, and put off her veil from her, and put on the garments of her widowhood. (20) And Judah sent the kid of the goats by the hand of his friend the Adullamite, to receive the pledge from the woman's hand: but he found her not. (21) Then he asked the men of her place, saying, Where is the [1] harlot, that was at Enaim by the way side? And they said, There hath been no [1] harlot here. (22) And he returned to Judah, and said, I have not found her; and also the men of the place said, There hath been no [1] harlot here. (23) And Judah said, Let her take it to her, lest we be put to shame: behold, I sent this kid, and thou hast not found her. (24) And it came to pass about three months after, that it was told Judah, saying, Tamar thy daughter in law hath played the harlot; and moreover, behold, she is with child by whoredom. And Judah said, Bring her forth, and let her be burnt. (25) When she was brought forth, she sent to her father in law, saying, By the man, whose these are, am I with child: and she said, Discern, I pray thee, whose are these, the signet, and the cords, and the staff. (26) And Judah acknowledged them, and said, She is more righteous than I; forasmuch as I gave her not to Shelah my son. And he knew her again no more. (27) And it came to pass in the time of her travail, that, behold, twins were in her womb. (28) And it came to pass, when she travailed, that one put out a hand: and the midwife took and bound upon his hand a scarlet thread, saying, This came out first. (29) And it came to pass, as he drew back his hand, that, behold, his brother came out: and she said, [2] Wherefore hast thou made a breach for thyself? therefore his name was called [3] Perez. (30) And afterward came out his brother, that had the scarlet thread upon his hand: and his name was called Zerah.

39 And Joseph was brought down to Egypt; and Potiphar, an officer of Pha-

---
[1] Heb. *kedeshah*, that is, a woman dedicated to impure heathen worship. See Deut. xxiii. 17, Hos. iv. 14.   [2] Or, *How hast thou made a breach! a breach be upon thee!*   [3] That is, *A breach.*

… … … … … …l. an Egyptian, bought him of the hand of the Ishmaelites, which had brought him down thither. (2) And the LORD was with Joseph, and he was a prosperous man; and he was in the house of his master the Egyptian. (3) And his master saw that the LORD was with him, and that the LORD made all that he did to prosper in his hand. (4) And Joseph found grace in his sight, and he ministered unto him: and he made him overseer over his house, and all that he had he put into his hand. (5) And it came to pass from the time that he made him overseer in his house, and over all that he had, that the LORD blessed the Egyptian's house for Joseph's sake; and the blessing of the LORD was upon all that he had, in the house and in the field. (6) And he left all that he had in Joseph's hand; and ¹ he knew not aught *that was* with him, save the bread which he did eat. And Joseph was comely, and well favoured. (7) And it came to pass after these things, that his master's wife cast her eyes upon Joseph; and she said, Lie with me. (8) But he refused, and said unto his master's wife, Behold, my master ² knoweth not what is with me in the house, and he hath put all that he hath to my hand: (9) ³ there is none greater in this house than I; neither hath he kept back any thing from me but thee, because thou art his wife: how then can I do this great wickedness, and sin against God? (10) And it came to pass, as she spake to Joseph day by day, that he hearkened not unto her, to lie by her, *or* to be with her. (11) And it came to pass about this time, that he went into the house to do his work; and there was none of the men of the house there within. (12) And she caught him by his garment, saying, Lie with me: and he left his garment in her hand, and fled, and got him out. (13) And it came to pass, when she saw that he had left his garment in her hand, and was fled forth, (14) that she called unto the men of her house, and spake unto them, saying, See, he hath brought in an Hebrew unto us to mock us; he came in unto me to lie with me, and I cried with a loud voice: (15) and it came to pass, when he heard that I lifted up my voice and cried, that he left his garment by me, and fled, and got him out. (16) And she laid up his garment by her, until his master came home. (17) And she spake unto him according to these words, saying, The Hebrew servant, which thou hast brought unto us, came in unto me to mock me: (18) and it came to pass, as I lifted up my voice and cried, that he left his garment by me, and fled out. (19) And it came to pass, when his master heard the words of his wife, which she spake unto him, saying, After this manner did thy servant to me; that his wrath was kindled. (20) And Joseph's master took him, and put him into the prison, the place where the king's prisoners were bound: and he was there in the prison. (21) But the LORD was with Joseph, and shewed kindness unto him, and gave him favour in the sight of the keeper of the prison. (22) And the keeper of the prison committed to Joseph's hand all the prisoners that were in the prison; and whatsoever they did there, he was the doer of it. (23) The keeper of the prison looked not to any thing that was under his hand, because the LORD was with him; and that which he did, the LORD made it to prosper.

40 And it came to pass after these things, that the butler of the king of Egypt and his baker offended their lord the king of Egypt. (2) And Pharaoh was wroth against his two officers, against the chief of the butlers, and against the chief of the bakers. (3) And he put them in ward in the house of the captain of the guard, into the prison, the place

---
¹ Or, *with him he knew not.* ² Or, *knoweth not with me what is &c.* ³ Or, *he is not.*

where Joseph was bound. (4) And the captain of the guard charged Joseph with them, and he ministered unto them: and they continued a season in ward. (5) And they dreamed a dream both of them, each man his dream, in one night, each man according to the interpretation of his dream, the butler and the baker of the king of Egypt, which were bound in the prison. (6) And Joseph came in unto them in the morning, and saw them, and, behold, they were sad. (7) And he asked Pharaoh's officers that were with him in ward in his master's house, saying, Wherefore look ye so sadly to-day? (8) And they said unto him, We have dreamed a dream, and there is none that can interpret it. And Joseph said unto them, Do not interpretations belong to God? tell it me, I pray you. (9) And the chief butler told his dream to Joseph, and said to him, In my dream, behold, a vine was before me; (10) and in the vine were three branches: and it was as though it budded, *and* its blossoms shot forth; *and* the clusters thereof brought forth ripe grapes: (11) and Pharaoh's cup was in my hand; and I took the grapes, and pressed them into Pharaoh's cup, and I gave the cup into Pharaoh's hand. (12) And Joseph said unto him, This is the interpretation of it: the three branches are three days; (13) within yet three days shall Pharaoh lift up thine head, and restore thee unto thine office: and thou shalt give Pharaoh's cup into his hand, after the former manner when thou wast his butler. (14) But have me in thy remembrance when it shall be well with thee, and shew kindness, I pray thee, unto me, and make mention of me unto Pharaoh, and bring me out of this house: (15) for indeed I was stolen away out of the land of the Hebrews: and here also have I done nothing that they should put me into the dungeon. (16) When the chief baker saw that the interpretation was good, he said unto Joseph, I also was in my dream, and, behold, three baskets of white bread were on my head: (17) and in the uppermost basket there was of all manner of bakemeats for Pharaoh; and the birds did eat them out of the basket upon my head. (18) And Joseph answered and said, This is the interpretation thereof: the three baskets are three days; (19) within yet three days shall Pharaoh lift up thy head from off thee, and shall hang thee on a tree; and the birds shall eat thy flesh from off thee. (20) And it came to pass the third day, which was Pharaoh's birthday, that he made a feast unto all his servants: and he lifted up the head of the chief butler and the head of the chief baker among his servants. (21) And he restored the chief butler unto his butlership again; and he gave the cup into Pharaoh's hand: (22) but he hanged the chief baker: as Joseph had interpreted to them. (23) Yet did not the chief butler remember Joseph, but forgat him.

41 And it came to pass at the end of two full years, that Pharaoh dreamed: and, behold, he stood by the [1] river. (2) And, behold, there came up out of the river seven kine, well favoured and fatfleshed; and they fed in the reed-grass. (3) And, behold, seven other kine came up after them out of the river, ill favoured and leanfleshed; and stood by the other kine upon the brink of the river. (4) And the ill favoured and leanfleshed kine did eat up the seven well favoured and fat kine. So Pharaoh awoke. (5) And he slept and dreamed a second time: and, behold, seven ears of corn came up upon one stalk, [2] rank and good. (6) And, behold, seven ears, thin and blasted with the east wind, sprung up after them. (7) And the thin ears swallowed up the seven [2] rank and full ears. And Pharaoh awoke, and, behold, it was a dream. (8) And it came

---

[1] Heb. *Yeor*, that is, the Nile.   [2] Heb. *fat*.

to pass in the morning that his spirit was troubled; and he sent and called for all the ¹ magicians of Egypt, and all the wise men thereof: and Pharaoh told them his dream; but there was none that could interpret them unto Pharaoh. (9) Then spake the chief butler unto Pharaoh, saying, I ² do remember my faults this day: (10) Pharaoh was wroth with his servants, and put me in ward in the house of the captain of the guard, me and the chief baker: (11) and we dreamed a dream in one night, I and he; we dreamed each man according to the interpretation of his dream. (12) And there was with us there a young man, an Hebrew, servant to the captain of the guard; and we told him, and he interpreted to us our dreams; to each man according to his dream he did interpret. (13) And it came to pass, as he interpreted to us, so it was; ³ me he restored unto mine office, and him he hanged. (14) Then Pharaoh sent and called Joseph, and they brought him hastily out of the dungeon: and he shaved himself, and changed his raiment, and came in unto Pharaoh. (15) And Pharaoh said unto Joseph, I have dreamed a dream, and there is none that can interpret it: and I have heard say of thee, that when thou hearest a dream thou canst interpret it. (16) And Joseph answered Pharaoh, saying, It is not in me: God shall give Pharaoh an answer of peace. (17) And Pharaoh spake unto Joseph, In my dream, behold, I stood upon the brink of the river: (18) and, behold, there came up out of the river seven kine, fatfleshed and well favoured; and they fed in the reed-grass: (19) and, behold, seven other kine came up after them, poor and very ill favoured and leanfleshed, such as I never saw in all the land of Egypt for badness: (20) and the lean and ill favoured kine did eat up the first seven fat kine: (21) and when they had eaten them up, it could not be known that they had eaten them; but they were still ill favoured, as at the beginning. So I awoke. (22) And I saw in my dream, and, behold, seven ears came up upon one stalk, full and good: (23) and, behold, seven ears, withered, thin, *and* blasted with the east wind, sprung up after them: (24) and the thin ears swallowed up the seven good ears: and I told it unto the magicians; but there was none that could declare it to me. (25) And Joseph said unto Pharaoh, The dream of Pharaoh is one: what God is about to do he hath declared unto Pharaoh. (26) The seven good kine are seven years; and the seven good ears are seven years: the dream is one. (27) And the seven lean and ill favoured kine that came up after them are seven years, and also the seven empty ears blasted with the east wind; they shall be seven years of famine. (28) That is the thing which I spake unto Pharaoh: What God is about to do he hath shewed unto Pharaoh. (29) Behold, there come seven years of great plenty throughout all the land of Egypt: (30) and there shall arise after them seven years of famine; and all the plenty shall be forgotten in the land of Egypt; and the famine shall consume the land; (31) and the plenty shall not be known in the land by reason of that famine which followeth; for it shall be very grievous. (32) And for that the dream was doubled unto Pharaoh twice, it is because the thing is established by God, and God will shortly bring it to pass. (33) Now therefore let Pharaoh look out a man discreet and wise, and set him over the land of Egypt. (34) Let Pharaoh do *this*, and let him appoint overseers over the land, and take up the fifth part of the land of Egypt in the seven plenteous years. (35) And let them gather all the food of these good years that come, and lay up corn under the hand of Pharaoh for food in the cities,

---

¹ Or, *sacred scribes*.   ² Or, *will make mention of*.   ³ Or, *I was restored . . . and he was hanged*.

and let them keep it. (36) And the food shall be for a store to the land against the seven years of famine, which shall be in the land of Egypt; that the land perish not through the famine. (37) And the thing was good in the eyes of Pharaoh, and in the eyes of all his servants. (38) And Pharaoh said unto his servants, Can we find such a one as this, a man in whom the spirit of God is? (39) And Pharaoh said unto Joseph, Forasmuch as God hath shewed thee all this, there is none so discreet and wise as thou: (40) thou shalt be over my house, and according unto thy word shall all my people [1] be ruled: only in the throne will I be greater than thou. (41) And Pharaoh said unto Joseph, See, I have set thee over all the land of Egypt. (42) And Pharaoh took off his signet ring from his hand, and put it upon Joseph's hand, and arrayed him in vestures of [2] fine linen, and put a gold chain about his neck; (43) and he made him to ride in the second chariot which he had; and they cried before him, [3] Bow the knee: and he set him over all the land of Egypt. (44) And Pharaoh said unto Joseph, I am Pharaoh, and without thee shall no man lift up his hand or his foot in all the land of Egypt. (45) And Pharaoh called Joseph's name Zaphenath-paneah, and he gave him to wife Asenath the daughter of Poti-phera priest of On. And Joseph went out over the land of Egypt. (46) And Joseph was thirty years old when he stood before Pharaoh king of Egypt. And Joseph went out from the presence of Pharaoh, and went throughout all the land of Egypt. (47) And in the seven plenteous years the earth brought forth by handfuls. (48) And he gathered up all the food of the seven years which were in the land of Egypt, and laid up the food in the cities: the food of the field, which was round about every city, laid he up in the same. (49) And Joseph laid up corn as the sand of the sea, very much, until he left numbering; for it was without number. (50) And unto Joseph were born two sons before the year of famine came, which Asenath the daughter of Poti-phera priest of On bare unto him. (51) And Joseph called the name of the firstborn [4] Manasseh: For, *said he*, God hath made me forget all my toil, and all my father's house. (52) And the name of the second called he [5] Ephraim: For God hath made me fruitful in the land of my affliction. (53) And the seven years of plenty, that was in the land of Egypt, came to an end. (54) And the seven years of famine began to come, according as Joseph had said: and there was famine in all lands; but in all the land of Egypt there was bread. (55) And when all the land of Egypt was famished, the people cried to Pharaoh for bread: and Pharaoh said unto all the Egyptians, Go unto Joseph; what he saith to you, do. (56) And the famine was over all the face of the earth: and Joseph opened all the storehouses, and sold unto the Egyptians; and the famine was sore in the land of Egypt. (57) And all countries came into Egypt to Joseph for to buy corn; because the famine was sore in all the earth.

42 Now Jacob saw that there was corn in Egypt, and Jacob said unto his sons, Why do ye look one upon another? (2) And he said, Behold, I have heard that there is corn in Egypt: get you down thither, and buy for us from thence; that we may live, and not die. (3) And Joseph's ten brethren went down to buy corn from Egypt. (4) But Benjamin, Joseph's brother, Jacob sent not with his brethren; for he said, Lest peradventure mischief befall him. (5) And the sons of Israel came to buy among those that came: for the famine was in the land of Canaan. (6) And Joseph was the gov-

---

[1] Or, *order themselves.* Or, *do homage.*   [2] Or, *cotton.*   [3] *Abrech*, probably an Egyptian word, similar in sound to the Hebrew word meaning *to kneel.*   [4] That is, *Making to forget.*   [5] From a Hebrew word signifying *to be fruitful.*

ernor over the land; he it was that sold to all the people of the land : and Joseph's brethren came, and bowed down themselves to him with their faces to the earth. (7) And Joseph saw his brethren, and he knew them, but made himself strange unto them, and spake roughly with them (and he said unto them, Whence come ye? And they said, From the land of Canaan to buy food.) (8) And Joseph knew his brethren, but they knew not him. (9) And Joseph remembered the dreams which he dreamed of them, and said unto them, Ye are spies ; to see the nakedness of the land ye are come. (10) And they said unto him, Nay, my lord, but to buy food are thy servants come. (11) We are all one man's sons; we are true men, thy servants are no spies. (12) And he said unto them, Nay, but to see the nakedness of the land ye are come. (13) And they said, We thy servants are twelve brethren, the sons of one man in the land of Canaan ; and, behold, the youngest is this day with our father, and one is not. (14) And Joseph said unto them, That is it that I spake unto you, saying, Ye are spies : (15) hereby ye shall be proved : by the life of Pharaoh ye shall not go forth hence, except your youngest brother come hither. (16) Send one of you, and let him fetch your brother, and ye shall be bound, that your words may be proved, whether there be truth in you : or else by the life of Pharaoh surely ye are spies. (17) And he put them all together into ward three days. (18) And Joseph said unto them the third day, This do, and live; for I fear God : (19) if ye be true men, let one of your brethren be bound in your prison house : but go ye, carry corn for the famine of your houses : (20) and bring your youngest brother unto me : so shall your words be verified, and ye shall not die. And they did so. (21) And they said one to another, We are verily guilty concerning our brother, in that we saw the distress of his soul, when he besought us, and we would not hear; therefore is this distress come upon us. (22) And Reuben answered them, saying, Spake I not unto you, saying, Do not sin against the child ; and ye would not hear? therefore also, behold, his blood is required. (23) And they knew not that Joseph understood them ; for there was an interpreter between them. (24) And he turned himself about from them, and wept ; and he returned to them, and spake to them, and took Simeon from among them, and bound him before their eyes. (25) Then Joseph commanded to fill their vessels with corn, and to restore every man's money into his sack, and to give them provision for the way : and thus was it done unto them. (26) And they laded their asses with their corn, and departed thence. (27) And as one of them opened his sack to give his ass provender in the lodging place, he espied his money ; and, behold, it was in the mouth of his sack. (28) And he said unto his brethren, My money is restored ; and, lo, it is even in my sack : and their heart failed them, and they turned trembling one to another, saying, What is this that God hath done unto us? (29) And they came unto Jacob their father unto the land of Canaan, and told him all that had befallen them ; saying, (30) The man, the lord of the land, spake roughly with us, and took us for spies of the country. (31) And we said unto him, We are true men ; we are no spies : (32) we be twelve brethren, sons of our father ; one is not, and the youngest is this day with our father in the land of Canaan. (33) And the man, the lord of the land, said unto us, Hereby shall I know that ye are true men ; leave one of your brethren with me, and take *corn for* the famine of your houses, and go your way : (34) and bring your youngest brother unto me : then shall I know that ye are no spies, but that ye are true men : so will I deliver you your brother, and ye shall traffick in the land. (35) And it came to pass as they emptied their sacks, that, behold, every man's bundle of money was in his sack: and when they and their father saw their bundles of money, they were afraid. (36) And Jacob their father said unto them, Me have ye bereaved of my children: Joseph is not, and Simeon is not, and ye will take Benjamin away: all these things are ¹against me. (37) And Reuben spake unto his father, saying, Slay my two sons, if I bring him not to thee: deliver him into my hand, and I will bring him to thee again. (38) And he said, My son shall not go down with you; for his brother is dead, and he only is left: if mischief befall him by the way in the which ye go, then shall ye bring down my gray hairs with sorrow to ² the grave.

43 And the famine was sore in the land. (2) And it came to pass, when they had eaten up the corn which they had brought out of Egypt, their father said unto them, Go again, buy us a little food. (3) And Judah spake unto him, saying, The man did solemnly protest unto us, saying, Ye shall not see my face, except your brother be with you. (4) If thou wilt send our brother with us, we will go down and buy thee food: (5) but if thou wilt not send him, we will not go down: for the man said unto us, Ye shall not see my face, except your brother be with you. (6) And Israel said, Wherefore dealt ye so ill with me, as to tell the man whether ye had yet a brother? (7) And they said, The man asked straitly concerning ourselves, and concerning our kindred, saying, Is your father yet alive? have ye *another* brother? and we told him according to the tenor of these words: could we in any wise know that he would say, Bring your brother down? (8) And Judah said unto Israel his father, Send the lad with me, and we will arise and go; that we may live, and not die, both we, and thou, and also our little ones. (9) I will be surety for him; of my hand shalt thou require him: if I bring him not unto thee, and set him before thee, then ³ let me bear the blame for ever: (10) for except we had lingered, surely we had now returned a second time. (11) And their father Israel said unto them, If it be so now, do this; take of the choice fruits of the land in your vessels, and carry down the man a present, a little ⁴ balm, and a little honey, spicery and myrrh, ⁵ nuts, and almonds: (12) and take double money in your hand; and the money that was returned in the mouth of your sacks carry again in your hand; peradventure it was an oversight: (13) take also your brother, and arise, go again unto the man: (14) and ⁶ God Almighty give you mercy before the man, that he may release unto you your other brother and Benjamin. And if I be bereaved of my children, I am bereaved. (15) And the men took that present, and they took double money in their hand, and Benjamin; and rose up, and went down to Egypt, and stood before Joseph. (16) And when Joseph saw Benjamin with them, he said to the steward of his house, Bring the men into the house, and slay, and make ready; for the men shall dine with me at noon. (17) And the man did as Joseph bade; and the man brought the men into Joseph's house. (18) And the men were afraid, because they were brought into Joseph's house; and they said, Because of the money that was returned in our sacks at the first time are we brought in; that he may ⁷ seek occasion against us, and fall upon us, and take us for bondmen, and our asses. (19) And they came near to the steward of Joseph's house, and they spake unto him at the

---

¹ Or, *upon*. ² Heb. *Sheol*. See ch. xxxvii. 35. ³ Heb. *I shall have sinned against thee for ever*. ⁴ See ch. xxxvii. 25. ⁵ That is, *pistachio nuts*. ⁶ Heb. *El Shaddai*. ⁷ Heb. *roll himself upon us*.

GENESIS.

door of the house, (20) and said, Oh my lord, we came indeed down at the first time to buy food: (21) and it came to pass, when we came to the lodging place, that we opened our sacks, and, behold, every man's money was in the mouth of his sack, our money in full weight: and we have brought it again in our hand. (22) And other money have we brought down in our hand to buy food: we know not who put our money in our sacks. (23) And he said, Peace be to you, fear not: your God, and the God of your father, hath given you treasure in your sacks: I had your money. And he brought Simeon out unto them. (24) And the man brought the men into Joseph's house, and gave them water, and they washed their feet; and he gave their asses provender. (25) And they made ready the present against Joseph came at noon: for they heard that they should eat bread there. (26) And when Joseph came home, they brought him the present which was in their hand into the house, and bowed down themselves to him to the earth. (27) And he asked them of their welfare, and said, Is your father well, the old man of whom ye spake? Is he yet alive? (28) And they said, Thy servant our father is well, he is yet alive. And they bowed the head, and made obeisance. (29) And he lifted up his eyes, and saw Benjamin his brother, his mother's son, and said, Is this your youngest brother, of whom ye spake unto me? And he said, God be gracious unto thee, my son. (30) And Joseph made haste; for his bowels did yearn upon his brother: and he sought where to weep; and he entered into his chamber, and wept there. (31) And he washed his face, and came out; and he refrained himself, and said, Set on bread. (32) And they set on for him by himself, and for them by themselves, and for the Egyptians, which did eat with him, by themselves: because the Egyptians might not eat bread with the Hebrews; for that is an abomination unto the Egyptians. (33) And they sat before him, the firstborn according to his birthright, and the youngest according to his youth: and the men marvelled one with another. (34) And [1] he took *and sent* messes unto them from before him: but Benjamin's mess was five times so much as any of theirs. And they drank, and [2] were merry with him.

44 And he commanded the steward of his house, saying, Fill the men's sacks with food, as much as they can carry, and put every man's money in his sack's mouth. (2) And put my cup, the silver cup, in the sack's mouth of the youngest, and his corn money. And he did according to the word that Joseph had spoken. (3) As soon as the morning was light, the men were sent away, they and their asses. (4) *And* when they were gone out of the city, and were not yet far off, Joseph said unto his steward, Up, follow after the men; and when thou dost overtake them, say unto them, Wherefore have ye rewarded evil for good? (5) Is not this it in which my lord drinketh, and whereby he indeed divineth? ye have done evil in so doing. (6) And he overtook them, and he spake unto them these words. (7) And they said unto him, Wherefore speaketh my lord such words as these? God forbid that thy servants should do such a thing. (8) Behold, the money, which we found in our sacks' mouths, we brought again unto thee out of the land of Canaan: how then should we steal out of thy lord's house silver or gold? (9) With whomsoever of thy servants it be found, let him die, and we also will be my lord's bondmen. (10) And he said, Now also let it be according unto your words: he with whom it is found shall be my bondman; and ye shall be blameless. (11) Then they hasted, and took down every man

---
[1] Or, *messes were taken.* [2] Heb. *drunk largely.*

his sack to the ground, and opened every man his sack. (12) And he searched, *and* began at the eldest, and left at the youngest: and the cup was found in Benjamin's sack. (13) Then they rent their clothes, and laded every man his ass, and returned to the city. (14) And Judah and his brethren came to Joseph's house; and he was yet there: and they fell before him on the ground. (15) And Joseph said unto them, What deed is this that ye have done? know ye not that such a man as I can indeed divine? (16) And Judah said, What shall we say unto my lord? what shall we speak? or how shall we clear ourselves? God hath found out the iniquity of thy servants: behold, we are my lord's bondmen, both we, and he also in whose hand the cup is found. (17) And he said, God forbid that I should do so: the man in whose hand the cup is found, he shall be my bondman; but as for you, get you up in peace unto your father.

(18) Then Judah came near unto him, and said, Oh my lord, let thy servant, I pray thee, speak a word in my lord's ears, and let not thine anger burn against thy servant: for thou art even as Pharaoh. (19) My lord asked his servants, saying, Have ye a father, or a brother? (20) And we said unto my lord, We have a father, an old man, and a child of his old age, a little one; and his brother is dead, and he alone is left of his mother, and his father loveth him. (21) And thou saidst unto thy servants, Bring him down unto me, that I may set mine eyes upon him. (22) And we said unto my lord, The lad cannot leave his father: for if he should leave his father, his father would die. (23) And thou saidst unto thy servants, Except your youngest brother come down with you, ye shall see my face no more. (24) And it came to pass when we came up unto thy servant my father, we told him the words of my lord. (25) And our father said, Go again, buy us a little food. (26) And we said, We cannot go down: if our youngest brother be with us, then will we go down: for we may not see the man's face, except our youngest brother be with us. (27) And thy servant my father said unto us, Ye know that my wife bare me two sons: (28) and the one went out from me, and I said, Surely he is torn in pieces; and I have not seen him since: (29) and if ye take this one also from me, and mischief befall him, ye shall bring down my gray hairs with [1] sorrow to [2] the grave. (30) Now therefore when I come to thy servant my father, and the lad be not with us; seeing that [3] his life is bound up in the lad's life; (31) it shall come to pass, when he seeth that the lad is not *with us*, that he will die: and thy servants shall bring down the gray hairs of thy servant our father with sorrow to [2] the grave. (32) For thy servant became surety for the lad unto my father, saying, If I bring him not unto thee, then shall I bear the blame to my father for ever. (33) Now therefore, let thy servant, I pray thee, abide instead of the lad a bondman to my lord; and let the lad go up with his brethren. (34) For how shall I go up to my father, and the lad be not with me? lest I see the evil that shall come on my father.

45 Then Joseph could not refrain himself before all them that stood by him; and he cried, Cause every man to go out from me. And there stood no man with him, while Joseph made himself known unto his brethren. (2) And he [4] wept aloud: and the Egyptians heard, and the house of Pharaoh heard. (3) And Joseph said unto his brethren, I am Joseph; doth my father yet live? And his brethren could not answer him; for

---

[1] Heb. *evil*.   [2] Heb. *Sheol*. See ch. xxxvii. 35.   [3] Or, *his soul is knit with the lad's soul*. See 1 Sam. xviii. 1.
[4] Heb. *gave forth his voice in weeping*.

they were troubled at his presence. (4) And Joseph said unto his brethren, Come near to me, I pray you. And they came near. And he said, I am Joseph your brother, whom ye sold into Egypt. (5) And now be not grieved, nor angry with yourselves, (that ye sold me hither;) for God did send me before you to preserve life. (6) For these two years hath the famine been in the land: and there are yet five years, in the which there shall be neither plowing nor harvest. (7) And God sent me before you to preserve you a remnant in the earth, and to save you alive ¹by a great deliverance. (8) So now it was not you that sent me hither, but God: and he hath made me a father to Pharaoh, and lord of all his house, and ruler over all the land of Egypt. (9) Haste ye, and go up to my father, and say unto him, Thus saith thy son Joseph, God hath made me lord of all Egypt: come down unto me, tarry not: (10) and thou shalt dwell in the land of Goshen, and thou shalt be near unto me, thou, and thy children, and thy children's children, and thy flocks, and thy herds, and all that thou hast: (11) and there will I nourish thee; for there are yet five years of famine; lest thou come to poverty, thou, and thy household, and all that thou hast. (12) And, behold, your eyes see, and the eyes of my brother Benjamin, that it is my mouth that speaketh unto you. (13) And ye shall tell my father of all my glory in Egypt, and of all that ye have seen; and ye shall haste and bring down my father hither. (14) And he fell upon his brother Benjamin's neck, and wept; and Benjamin wept upon his neck. (15) And he kissed all his brethren, and wept upon them: and after that his brethren talked with him.

(16) And the fame thereof was heard in Pharaoh's house, saying, Joseph's brethren are come: and it pleased Pharaoh well, and his servants. (17) And Pharaoh said unto Joseph, Say unto thy brethren, This do ye; lade your beasts, and go, get you unto the land of Canaan; (18) and take your father and your households, and come unto me: and I will give you the good of the land of Egypt, and ye shall eat the fat of the land. (19) Now thou art commanded, this do ye; take you wagons out of the land of Egypt for your little ones, and for your wives, and bring your father, and come. (20) Also regard not your stuff: for the good of all the land of Egypt is yours. (21) And the sons of Israel did so: and Joseph gave them wagons, according to the commandment of Pharaoh, and gave them provision for the way. (22) To all of them he gave each man changes of raiment; but to Benjamin he gave three hundred pieces of silver, and five changes of raiment. (23) And to his father he sent after this manner; ten asses laden with the good things of Egypt, and ten she-asses laden with corn and bread and victual for his father by the way. (24) So he sent his brethren away, and they departed: and he said unto them, See that ye fall not out by the way. (25) And they went up out of Egypt, and came into the land of Canaan unto Jacob their father. (26) And they told him, saying, Joseph is yet alive, and he is ruler over all the land of Egypt. And his heart fainted, for he believed them not. (27) And they told him all the words of Joseph, which he had said unto them: and when he saw the wagons which Joseph had sent to carry him, the spirit of Jacob their father revived: (28) and Israel said, It is enough; Joseph my son is yet alive: I will go and see him before I die.

46 And Israel took his journey with all that he had, and came to Beer-sheba, and offered sacrifices unto the God of his father Isaac. (2) And God spake unto

---

¹ Or, *to be a great company that escape*.

Israel in the visions of the night, and said, Jacob, Jacob. And he said, Here am I. (3) And he said, I am God, the God of thy father: fear not to go down into Egypt; for I will there make of thee a great nation: (4) I will go down with thee into Egypt; and I will also surely bring thee up again: and Joseph shall put his hand upon thine eyes. (5) And Jacob rose up from Beer-sheba: and the sons of Israel carried Jacob their father, and their little ones, and their wives, in the wagons which Pharaoh had sent to carry him. (6) And they took their cattle, and their goods, which they had gotten in the land of Canaan, and came into Egypt, Jacob, and all his seed with him: (7) his sons, and his sons' sons with him, his daughters, and his sons' daughters, and all his seed brought he with him into Egypt.

(8) And these are the names of the children of Israel, which came into Egypt, Jacob and his sons: Reuben, Jacob's firstborn. (9) And the sons of Reuben; Hanoch, and Pallu, and Hezron, and Carmi. (10) And the sons of Simeon; [1] Jemuel, and Jamin, and Ohad, and [2] Jachin, and [3] Zohar, and Shaul the son of a Canaanitish woman. (11) And the sons of Levi; [4] Gershon, Kohath, and Merari. (12) And the sons of Judah; Er, and Onan, and Shelah, and Perez, and Zerah: but Er and Onan died in the land of Canaan. And the sons of Perez were Hezron and Hamul. (13) And the sons of Issachar; Tola, and [5] Puvah, and Iob, and Shimron. (14) And the sons of Zebulun; Sered, and Elon, and Jahleel. (15) These are the sons of Leah, which she bare unto Jacob in Paddan-aram, with his daughter Dinah: all the souls of his sons and his daughters were thirty and three. (16) And the sons of Gad; [6] Ziphion, and Haggi, Shuni, and [7] Ezbon, Eri, and Arodi, and Areli. (17) And the sons of Asher: Imnah, and Ishvah, and Ishvi, and Beriah, and Serah their sister: and the sons of Beriah; Heber, and Malchiel. (18) These are the sons of Zilpah, which Laban gave to Leah his daughter, and these she bare unto Jacob, even sixteen souls. (19) The sons of Rachel Jacob's wife; Joseph and Benjamin. (20) And unto Joseph in the land of Egypt were born Manasseh and Ephraim, which Asenath the daughter of Poti-phera priest of On bare unto him. (21) And the sons of Benjamin; Bela, and Becher, and Ashbel, Gera, and Naaman, [9] Ehi, and Rosh, [10] Muppim, and [11] Huppim, and Ard. (22) These are the sons of Rachel, which were born to Jacob: all the souls were fourteen. (23) And the sons of Dan; [12] Hushim. (24) And the sons of Naphtali; [13] Jahzeel, and Guni, and Jezer, and [14] Shillem. (25) These are the sons of Bilhah, which Laban gave unto Rachel his daughter, and these she bare unto Jacob: all the souls were seven. (26) All the [15] souls that came with Jacob into Egypt, which came out of his loins, besides Jacob's sons' wives, all the souls were threescore and six: (27) and the sons of Joseph, which were born to him in Egypt, were two souls: all the souls of the house of Jacob, which came into Egypt, were threescore and ten.

(28) And he sent Judah before him unto Joseph, to shew the way before him unto Goshen; and they came into the land of Goshen. (29) And Joseph made ready his chariot, and went up to meet Israel his father, to Goshen; and he presented himself unto him, and fell on his neck, and wept on his neck a good while. (30) And Israel said unto Joseph, Now let me die, since I have seen thy face, that thou art yet alive. (31) And Joseph said unto

---

[1] In Num. xxvi. 12, 1 Chr. iv. 24, *Nemuel*. [2] In 1 Chr. iv. 24, *Jarib*. [3] In Num. xxvi. 13, 1 Chr. iv. 24, *Zerah*. [4] In 1 Chr. vi. 16, *Gershom*. [5] In 1 Chr. vii. 1, *Puah, Jashub*. See Num. xxvi. 23, 24. [6] In Num. xxvi. 15, *Zephon*. [7] In Num. xxvi. 16, *Ozni*. [8] In 1 Chr. xxvi. 17, *Arod*. [9] In Num. xxvi. 38, *Ahiram*. [10] In Num. xxvi. 39, *Shephupham*, in 1 Chr. vii. 12, *Shuppim*. [11] In Num. xxvi. 39, *Hupham*. [12] In Num. xxvi. 42, *Shuham*. [13] In 1 Chr. vii. 13, *Jahziel*. [14] In 1 Chr. vii. 13, *Shallum*. [15] Or, *souls belonging to Jacob that came*.

his brethren, and unto his father's house. I will go up, and tell Pharaoh, and will say unto him, My brethren, and my father's house, which were in the land of Canaan, are come unto me; (32) and the men are shepherds, for they have been keepers of cattle; and they have brought their flocks, and their herds, and all that they have. (33) And it shall come to pass, when Pharaoh shall call you, and shall say, What is your occupation? (34) that ye shall say, Thy servants have been keepers of cattle from our youth even until now, both we, and our fathers: that ye may dwell in the land of Goshen; for every shepherd is an abomination unto the Egyptians.

47 Then Joseph went in and told Pharaoh, and said, My father and my brethren, and their flocks, and their herds, and all that they have, are come out of the land of Canaan; and, behold, they are in the land of Goshen. (2) And from among his brethren he took five men, and presented them unto Pharaoh. (3) And Pharaoh said unto his brethren, What is your occupation? And they said unto Pharaoh, Thy servants are shepherds, both we, and our fathers. (4) And they said unto Pharaoh, To sojourn in the land are we come; for there is no pasture for thy servants' flocks; for the famine is sore in the land of Canaan: now therefore, we pray thee, let thy servants dwell in the land of Goshen. (5) And Pharaoh spake unto Joseph, saying, Thy father and thy brethren are come unto thee: (6) the land of Egypt is before thee; in the best of the land make thy father and thy brethren to dwell; in the land of Goshen let them dwell: and if thou knowest any ¹ able men among them, then make them rulers over my cattle. (7) And Joseph brought in Jacob his father, and set him before Pharaoh: and Jacob blessed Pharaoh. (8) And Pharaoh said unto Jacob, How many are the days of the years of thy life? (9) And Jacob said unto Pharaoh, The days of the years of my ² pilgrimage are an hundred and thirty years: few and evil have been the days of the years of my life, and they have not attained unto the days of the years of the life of my fathers in the days of their ² pilgrimage. (10) And Jacob blessed Pharaoh, and went out from the presence of Pharaoh. (11) And Joseph placed his father and his brethren, and gave them a possession in the land of Egypt, in the best of the land, in the land of Rameses, as Pharaoh had commanded. (12) And Joseph nourished his father, and his brethren, and all his father's household, with bread, ³ according to their families.

(13) And there was no bread in all the land; for the famine was very sore, so that the land of Egypt and the land of Canaan fainted by reason of the famine. (14) And Joseph gathered up all the money that was found in the land of Egypt, and in the land of Canaan, for the corn which they bought: and Joseph brought the money into Pharaoh's house. (15) And when the money was all spent in the land of Egypt, and in the land of Canaan, all the Egyptians came unto Joseph, and said, Give us bread: for why should we die in thy presence? for *our* money faileth. (16) And Joseph said, Give your cattle; and I will give you for your cattle, if money fail. (17) And they brought their cattle unto Joseph: and Joseph gave them bread in exchange for the horses, and for the ⁴ flocks, and for the herds, and for the asses: and he ⁵ fed them with bread in exchange for all their cattle for that year. (18) And when that year was ended, they came unto him the second year, and said unto him, We will not hide from my lord, how that our

---

¹ Or, *men of activity.* ² Or, *sojournings.* ³ Or, *according to the number of their little ones.* ⁴ Heb. *cattle of the flocks, and for the cattle of the herds.* ⁵ Heb. *led them as a shepherd.*

money is all spent; and the herds of cattle are my lord's; there is nought left in the sight of my lord, but our bodies, and our lands: (19) wherefore should we die before thine eyes, both we and our land? buy us and our land for bread, and we and our land will be servants unto Pharaoh: and give us seed, that we may live, and not die, and that the land be not desolate. (20) So Joseph bought all the land of Egypt for Pharaoh; for the Egyptians sold every man his field, because the famine was sore upon them: and the land became Pharaoh's. (21) And as for the people, [1] he removed them [2] to the cities from one end of the border of Egypt even to the other end thereof. (22) Only the land of the priests bought he not: for the priests had a portion from Pharaoh, and did eat their portion which Pharaoh gave them; wherefore they sold not their land. (23) Then Joseph said unto the people, Behold, I have bought you this day and your land for Pharaoh: lo, here is seed for you, and ye shall sow the land. (24) And it shall come to pass at the ingatherings, that ye shall give a fifth unto Pharaoh, and four parts shall be your own, for seed of the field, and for your food, and for them of your households, and for food for your little ones. (25) And they said, Thou hast saved our lives: let us find grace in the sight of my lord, and we will be Pharaoh's servants. (26) And Joseph made it a statute concerning the land of Egypt unto this day, that Pharaoh should have the fifth; only the land of the priests alone became not Pharaoh's. (27) And Israel dwelt in the land of Egypt, in the land of Goshen; and they gat them possessions therein, and were fruitful, and multiplied exceedingly.

(28) And Jacob lived in the land of Egypt seventeen years: so the days of Jacob, the years of his life, were an hundred forty and seven years. (29) And the time drew near that Israel must die: and he called his son Joseph, and said unto him, If now I have found grace in thy sight, put, I pray thee, thy hand under my thigh, and deal kindly and truly with me; bury me not, I pray thee, in Egypt: (30) but when I sleep with my fathers, thou shalt carry me out of Egypt, and bury me in their buryingplace. And he said, I will do as thou hast said. (31) And he said, Swear unto me: and he sware unto him. And Israel bowed himself upon the bed's head.

48 And it came to pass after these things, that one said to Joseph, Behold, thy father is sick: and he took with him his two sons, Manasseh and Ephraim. (2) And one told Jacob, and said, Behold, thy son Joseph cometh unto thee: and Israel strengthened himself, and sat upon the bed. (3) And Jacob said unto Joseph, [3] God Almighty appeared unto me at Luz in the land of Canaan, and blessed me, (4) and said unto me, Behold, I will make thee fruitful, and multiply thee, and I will make of thee a company of peoples; and will give this land to thy seed after thee for an everlasting possession. (5) And now thy two sons, which were born unto thee in the land of Egypt before I came unto thee into Egypt, are mine; Ephraim and Manasseh, even as Reuben and Simeon, shall be mine. (6) And thy issue, which thou [4] begettest after them, shall be thine; they shall be called after the name of their brethren in their inheritance. (7) And as for me, when I came from Paddan, Rachel died [5] by me in the land of Canaan in the way, when there was still some way to come unto Ephrath: and I buried her there in the way to Ephrath (the same is Beth-lehem). (8) And Israel beheld Joseph's sons, and said, Who are these? (9) And Joseph said

---

[1] According to Samar., Sept. and Vulg., *he made bondmen of them, from &c.*   [2] Or, *according to their cities.*
[3] Heb. *El Shaddai.*   [4] Or, *hast begotten.*   [5] Or, *to my sorrow.*

unto his father, They are my sons, whom God hath given me here. And he said, Bring them, I pray thee, unto me, and I will bless them. (10) Now the eyes of Israel were dim for age, so that he could not see. And he brought them near unto him; and he kissed them, and embraced them. (11) And Israel said unto Joseph, I had not thought to see thy face: and, lo, God hath let me see thy seed also. (12) And Joseph brought them out from between his knees; and he bowed himself with his face to the earth. (13) And Joseph took them both, Ephraim in his right hand toward Israel's left hand, and Manasseh in his left hand toward Israel's right hand, and brought them near unto him. (14) And Israel stretched out his right hand, and laid it upon Ephraim's head, who was the younger, and his left hand upon Manasseh's head, ¹ guiding his hands wittingly; for Manasseh was the first born. (15) And he blessed Joseph, and said, The God before whom my fathers Abraham and Isaac did walk, the God which hath fed me all my life long unto this day, (16) the angel which hath redeemed me from all evil, bless the lads; and let my name be named on them, and the name of my fathers Abraham and Isaac; and let them grow into a multitude in the midst of the earth. (17) And when Joseph saw that his father laid his right hand upon the head of Ephraim, it displeased him: and he held up his father's hand, to remove it from Ephraim's head unto Manasseh's head. (18) And Joseph said unto his father, Not so, my father: for this is the firstborn; put thy right hand upon his head. (19) And his father refused, and said, I know *it*, my son, I know *it*: he also shall become a people, and he also shall be great: howbeit his younger brother shall be greater than he, and his seed shall become ² a multitude of nations.

(20) And he blessed them that day, saying, ³ In thee shall Israel bless, saying, God make thee as Ephraim and as Manasseh: and he set Ephraim before Manasseh. (21) And Israel said unto Joseph, Behold, I die: but God shall be with you, and bring you again unto the land of your fathers. (22) Moreover I have given to thee one ⁴ portion above thy brethren, which I took out of the hand of the Amorite with my sword and with my bow.

49 And Jacob called unto his sons, and said: Gather yourselves together, that I may tell you that which shall befall you in the latter days.

(2) Assemble yourselves, and hear, ye sons of Jacob;
And hearken unto Israel your father.
(3) Reuben, thou art my firstborn,
my might, and the beginning of my strength;
The excellency of dignity, and the excellency of power:
(4) ⁵ Unstable as water, thou shalt not have the excellency;
Because thou wentest up to thy father's bed;
Then defiledst thou it: he went up to my couch.
(5) Simeon and Levi are brethren;
Weapons of ⁶ violence are their swords.
(6) O my soul, come thou not into their council;
Unto their assembly, mine honour, be not thou united:
For in their anger they slew a man,
And in their selfwill they houghed ¹¹ an ox.
(7) Cursed be their anger, for it was fierce;
And their wrath, for it was cruel:
I will divide them in Jacob,
And scatter them in Israel.
(8) Judah, thee shall thy brethren praise:

---

¹ Or, *crossing his hands*. ² Heb. *fulness*. ³ Or, *By*. ⁴ Or, *mountain slope*. Heb. *shechem, shoulder*. ⁵ Or, *firstfruits*. ⁶ Or, *Bubbling over*. ⁷ Or, *have not thou*. ⁸ Or, *compacts*. ⁹ Or, *secret*. ¹⁰ Or, *men*. ¹¹ Or, *oxen*.

GENESIS.

Thy hand shall be on the neck of thine
enemies ;
Thy father's sons shall bow down before thee.
(9) Judah is a lion's whelp ;
From the prey, my son, thou art gone up :
He stooped down, he couched as a lion,
And as a lioness ; who shall rouse him up?
(10) The sceptre shall not depart from
Judah,
Nor ¹ the ruler's staff from between his
feet,
² Until Shiloh come ;
And unto him shall the obedience of the
peoples be.
(11) Binding his foal unto the vine,
And his ass's colt unto the choice vine ;
He hath washed his garments in wine,
And his vesture in the blood of grapes :
(12) His eyes shall be red with wine,
And his teeth white with milk.
(13) Zebulun shall dwell at the ⁴ haven
of the sea :
And he shall be for an ⁴ haven of ships ;
And his border shall be ⁴ upon Zidon.
(14) Issachar is a strong ass,
Couching down between the sheepfolds :
(15) And he saw ⁵ a resting place that
it was good,
And the land that it was pleasant ;
And he bowed his shoulder to bear,
And became a servant under taskwork.
(16) Dan shall judge his people,
As one of the tribes of Israel.
(17) Dan shall be a serpent in the way,
An ⁶ adder in the path,
That biteth the horse's heels.
So that his rider falleth backward.
(18) I have waited for thy salvation, O
LORD.
(19) Gad, ⁷ a troop ⁸ shall press upon
him :
But he shall press upon their heel.

(20) ⁹ Out of Asher his bread shall
be fat,
And he shall yield royal dainties.
(21) Naphtali is a hind let loose :
He giveth goodly words.
(22) Joseph is ¹⁰ a fruitful bough,
A fruitful bough by a fountain ;
His ¹¹ branches run over the wall.
(23) The archers have sorely grieved
him,
And shot at him, and persecuted him :
(24) But his bow abode in strength,
And the arms of his hands were made
¹² strong,
By the hands of the Mighty One of
Jacob,
(¹³ From thence is the shepherd, the
stone of Israel,)
(25) Even by the God of thy father,
who shall help thee,
And by the Almighty, who shall bless
thee,
With blessings of heaven above,
Blessings of the deep that coucheth beneath,
Blessings of the breasts, and of the
womb,
(26) The blessings of thy father
Have prevailed above ¹⁴ the blessings of
my progenitors
Unto the utmost bound of the everlasting hills :
They shall be on the head of Joseph,
And on the crown of the head of him
¹⁵ that was separate from his brethren.
(27) Benjamin is a wolf that ravineth :
In the morning he shall devour the prey,
And at even he shall divide the spoil.
(28) All these are the twelve tribes of
Israel : and this is it that their father
spake unto them **and blessed them** ; every

---
¹ Or, a lawgiver. ² Or, Till he come to Shiloh, having the obedience of the peoples. Or, as read by the Sept., Until that which is his shall come &c. Another ancient rendering is, Till he come whose it is &c. ³ Heb. beach.
⁴ Or, by. ⁵ Or, rest. ⁶ Or, horned snake. ⁷ Heb. gedud, a marauding band. ⁸ Heb. gud, to press. ⁹ According to some ancient versions, Asher, his bread &c. ¹⁰ Heb. the son of a fruitful tree. ¹¹ Heb. daughters.
¹² Or, active. ¹³ Or, From thence, from the shepherd. Or, as otherwise read, By the name of the shepherd.
¹⁴ According to some ancient authorities, the blessings of the ancient mountains, the desire (or, desirable things) of the everlasting hills. ¹⁵ Or, that is prince among.

one according to his blessing he blessed them. (29) And he charged them, and said unto them, I am to be gathered unto my people: bury me with my fathers in the cave that is in the field of Ephron the Hittite, (30) in the cave that is in the field of Machpelah, which is before Mamre, in the land of Canaan, which Abraham bought with the field from Ephron the Hittite for a possession of a buryingplace: (31) there they buried Abraham and Sarah his wife; there they buried Isaac and Rebekah his wife; and there I buried Leah: (32) the field and the cave that is therein, which was purchased from the children of Heth. (33) And when Jacob made an end of charging his sons, he gathered up his feet into the bed, and yielded up the ghost, and was gathered unto his people. 50 And Joseph fell upon his father's face, and wept upon him, and kissed him. (2) And Joseph commanded his servants the physicians to embalm his father: and the physicians embalmed Israel. (3) And forty days were fulfilled for him; for so are fulfilled the days of embalming: and the Egyptians wept for him threescore and ten days.

(4) And when the days of weeping for him were past, Joseph spake unto the house of Pharaoh, saying, If now I have found grace in your eyes, speak, I pray you, in the ears of Pharaoh, saying, (5) My father made me swear, saying, Lo, I die: in my grave which I [1]have digged for me in the land of Canaan, there shalt thou bury me. Now therefore let me go up, I pray thee, and bury my father, and I will come again. (6) And Pharaoh said, Go up, and bury thy father, according as he made thee swear. (7) And Joseph went up to bury his father: and with him went up all the servants of Pharaoh, the elders of his house, and all the elders of the land of Egypt, (8) and all the house of Joseph, and his brethren, and his father's house: only their little ones, and their flocks, and their herds, they left in the land of Goshen. (9) And there went up with him both chariots and horsemen: and it was a very great company. (10) And they came to the threshing-floor of Atad, which is beyond Jordan, and there they lamented with a very great and sore lamentation: and he made a mourning for his father seven days. (11) And when the inhabitants of the land, the Canaanites, saw the mourning in the floor of Atad, they said, This is a grievous [2]mourning to the Egyptians: wherefore the name of it was called Abelmizraim, which is beyond Jordan. (12) And his sons did unto him according as he commanded them: (13) for his sons carried him into the land of Canaan, and buried him in the cave of the field of Machpelah, which Abraham bought with the field, for a possession of a buryingplace, of Ephron the Hittite, before Mamre.

(14) And Joseph returned into Egypt, he, and his brethren, and all that went up with him to bury his father, after he had buried his father. (15) And when Joseph's brethren saw that their father was dead, they said, It may be that Joseph will hate us, and will fully requite us all the evil which we did unto him. (16) And they sent a message unto Joseph, saying, Thy father did command before he died, saying, (17) So shall ye say unto Joseph, Forgive, I pray thee now, the transgression of thy brethren, and their sin, for that they did unto thee evil: and now, we pray thee, forgive the transgression of the servants of the God of thy father. And Joseph wept when they spake unto him. (18) And his brethren also went and fell down before his face; and they said, Behold, we be thy servants. (19) And Joseph said unto them, Fear

---
[1] Or, *bought*. [2] Heb. *ebel*.

not: for am I in the place of God? (20) And as for you, ye meant evil against me; but God meant it for good, to bring to pass, as it is this day, to save much people alive. (21) Now therefore fear ye not: I will nourish you, and your little ones. And he comforted them, and spake ¹ kindly unto them.

(22) And Joseph dwelt in Egypt, he, and his father's house: and Joseph lived an hundred and ten years. (23) And Joseph saw Ephraim's children of the third generation: the children also of Machir the son of Manasseh were born upon Joseph's knees. (24) And Joseph said unto his brethren, I die: but God will surely visit you, and bring you up out of this land unto the land which he sware to Abraham, to Isaac, and to Jacob. (25) And Joseph took an oath of the children of Israel, saying, God will surely visit you, and ye shall carry up my bones from hence. (26) So Joseph died, being an hundred and ten years old: and they embalmed him, and he was put in a coffin in Egypt.

---

¹ Heb. *to their heart.*

www.ingramcontent.com/pod-product-compliance
Lightning Source LLC
Chambersburg PA
CBHW020235090426
42735CB00010B/1698